Set design by Lauren Helpern

Photo by Jim Baldassare

A scene from the Back House Productions presentation of *Savages*.

SAVAGES

BY ANNE NELSON

★

★

DRAMATISTS
PLAY SERVICE
INC.

SAVAGES
Copyright © 2007, Anne Nelson

All Rights Reserved

SPECIAL NOTE

Anyone receiving permission to produce SAVAGES is required to give credit to the Author as sole and exclusive Author of the Play on the title page of all programs distributed in connection with performances of the Play and in all instances in which the title of the Play appears for purposes of advertising, publicizing or otherwise exploiting the Play and/or a production thereof. The name of the Author must appear on a separate line, in which no other name appears, immediately beneath the title and in size of type equal to 50% of the size of the largest, most prominent letter used for the title of the Play. No person, firm or entity may receive credit larger or more prominent than that accorded the Author. The following acknowledgments must appear on the title page in all programs distributed in connection with performances of the Play:

Savages was written at the New Harmony Playwriting Project,
New Harmony, Indiana, in 2004, where it had its first reading.
Additional work was completed in a New River Dramatists residency.

SAVAGES was originally presented as a PlayFest Workshop Production
at the Orlando-UCF Shakespeare Festival (Jim Helsinger, Artistic Director).

SAVAGES premiered in New York City on March 9, 2006.
It was produced by Back House Productions
(Thomas Kail, Artistic Director; Anthony Veneziale, Associate Artistic Director),
in association with Modern Projects, Perry Silver and James West.

SPECIAL NOTE ON MUSIC

A CD with cue sheet of the sound design and original music composed by Jill BC DuBoff is available through the Play Service for $35.00, plus shipping. The nonprofessional fee for the use of this music is $20.00 per performance.

*To my father
and the woman in Dublin*

ACKNOWLEDGMENTS

I would like to thank the following servicemen and veterans for their assistance with military questions: Dan Lauria, Dan McSweeney, Kevin O'Kane, and John Manley (USMC); and Jay Parker and Ron Mangum (US Army). For background on the Philippines: Mayang Grenough and Helen Graham of Maryknoll, and Dr. Wilmo C. Orejola of Samar.

I also offer my gratitude to Thomas Kail, Jane Owen, Margaret Nolan, Anthony Veneziale, Nevin Steinberg, Mark St. Germaine, John Hill, Chris Jorie, Patrick Flick, Jay Turton, Beau Willimon, the Quantico archives, Allen Hubby and the Drama Book Shop, and the Lawton Community Theatre.

SAVAGES was born and had its first reading at the New Harmony Project in Indiana, and would not have been possible without New Harmony's support and encouragement. Additional work on the play was done in residence at New River Dramatists in North Carolina.

SAVAGES was originally presented as a PlayFest Workshop Production at the Orlando-UCF Shakespeare Festival (Jim Helsinger, Artistic Director) in Orlando, Florida.

SAVAGES premiered in New York, produced by Back House Productions (Thomas Kail, Artistic Director; Anthony Veneziale, Associate Artistic Director), in association with Modern Projects, Perry Silver and James West. It was directed by Chris Jorie; the set design was by Lauren Helpern; the lighting design was by Betsy Adams; the costume design was by Rebecca Bernstein; the sound design was by Jill BC DuBoff; and the production stage manager was Samone B. Weissman. The cast was as follows:

MAJOR LITTLETON WALLER .... James Matthew Ryan
MARIDOL AMAYA .... Julie Danao-Salkin
CORPORAL JOHN HANLEY .... Brett Holland
GENERAL ADNA CHAFFEE .... Jim Howard

CHARACTERS

GENERAL ADNA CHAFFEE, U.S. Army, in his 50s
CORPORAL JOHN HANLEY, U.S. Army, in his 20s
MARIDOL AMAYA, in her 20s
MAJOR LITTLETON WALLER, U.S. Marines, in his 40s

PLACE

The Philippines.

TIME

1902.

SAVAGES

Scene 1

We Will Not Discuss the Trial

CHAFFEE. We had every advantage — men, supplies, firepower. Half a their weapons were antiques and the other half were home-made. You wanted to laugh — 'til one of 'em took a piece a you with it. We tried to fight clean — everyone does at the start. But it ain't so easy. An old lady gives you water one day, and she's tipping off an ambush the next. You storm a nest a snipers ... and damned if it ain't a bunch of twelve-year-old boys playing soldier. *(Beat.)* Finally General Sheridan says: "Enough's enough. Burn it down." *(Simply.)* So we did. Everything in sight.
HANLEY. Yes sir! *(Pause.)* Did it work?
CHAFFEE. It sure did. Starved 'em out. Y'know, for the longest time, all I wanted to do was hightail it back to Ohio. But you get used to the life. The men you're serving with — well, you'd do any-thing for 'em. And you never feel quite so — *electric* — as the hour before battle.
HANLEY. Yes Sir!
CHAFFEE. Y' look out on a clear Virginia morning, with the mist ... and smoke ... rising over the Shenandoah ... *(Chaffee comes back to reality, looking towards the window.)* Can't say a *Manila* morning's half so fine.
HANLEY. No, sir, I reckon not. *(Pause.)* General Chaffee, if you'll pardon me for asking — how old were you in the Virginia campaign?
CHAFFEE. Oh ... just past twenty. *(He gives Hanley a long look.)*
HANLEY. And here you are commanding the whole damn Philippines!
CHAFFEE. That's right, son. Rose right up through the ranks. *(Abruptly.)* But that's ancient history. We got us a war to fight.

HANLEY. You want me to open the shutters?

CHAFFEE. *(He nods.)* Air it out. *(Hanley opens the shutters wide and bright tropical light floods the room. Chaffee goes to the window and gazes out to the street. Sounds of voices, wagons, and river traffic are heard.)* Look at them — the teeming horde. How're you sposed to read their faces? Sullen as a Baptist in a barroom. Their language sounds like monkey chatter. "Oh-oh! Oh-oh!" [Rhymes with "Go go."] *(Instructively, to Hanley.)* Listen up, soldier. If they wave their bolos around and curse, don't you worry, it's just for show. It's the smile you gotta watch out for. That sugar sweet smile. "Yes sir! No prob-ee sir!" That's when they're out for blood.

HANLEY. *(Attentively.)* Yes sir!

CHAFFEE. This place makes you appreciate the Spaniards — they were so damn cooperative. Wore their uniforms, lined up for battle — agreed to kill and be killed like gentlemen. *(Beat.)* Well, a soldier can't choose his enemies. Just his wife.

HANLEY. *(He pauses to consider.)* Yessir.

CHAFFEE. *(Turning back to the room.)* Let's see. The court martial adjourns at four. The Major should be here soon.

HANLEY. *(Pulling out a pocket watch.)* It's almost four now, sir.

CHAFFEE. The bed looks good. No holes in the netting … You got quinine?

HANLEY. On the shelf, sir. Eight bottles. *(Looking over to the shelf.)* Damn, we got us a whole darn hospital!

CHAFFEE. Well, that's fine, but quinine's the point. Two grams a day. But watch out — it's nasty stuff.

HANLEY. How's that, General Chaffee?

CHAFFEE. Affects a man's reason. And that's on top of the fever. Half a Waller's men were delirious when they got back from Samar.

HANLEY. Shouldn't he be in the hospital?

CHAFFEE. *(Sharply.)* That's as may be, but then he couldn't a stood trial.

HANLEY. No sir.

CHAFFEE. And our Marine *did* insist on his trial. Why couldn't he just plead guilty and take his medicine? But no — he was gonna "clear his name"!

HANLEY. Did he, sir?

CHAFFEE. *(Pointedly.)* They call him the "Butcher of Samar." His prisoners are dead and they're not comin' back. *(Beat. With the beginnings of sympathy.)* Waller did lose a lot of men in the massacre last September. But dammit, we all did — you can't just go around shootin' prisoners.

HANLEY. No sir! *(Tentatively.)* But why's he comin' here?

CHAFFEE. He can't stay in the brig, that's why. The man looked like death warmed over in court today. If he collapses tomorrow they'll call a mistrial — that's the last thing I need. Give 'im one good night's rest and get it over with — so I can get Washington off my back! *(He looks around the room grimly.)* What about the girl?

HANLEY. She's here, sir. In the servant's quarters.

CHAFFEE. She's a nurse?

HANLEY. Not ... exactly? But she's been working in the wards. The surgeon says she's real good with the wounded. Speaks some English.

CHAFFEE. She's a native?

HANLEY. It was hard enough to get *her.* Everyone's shorthanded from — Ba-Ba-tang —

CHAFFEE. Batangas. I know. Shorthanded! Huh! Coolies everywhere and not a one you can trust.

HANLEY. Did you want to look her over, sir?

CHAFFEE. Might as well.

HANLEY. Hey there! You! The General wants to see you. Chop chop! *(A pause. Maridol appears in the doorway, hands folded and eyes downcast.)*

CHAFFEE. Why, you're just a lil' scrap of a thing. Barely big enough to lift a bedpan. What's your name, girl?

MARIDOL. *(Stoically.)* Maridol Amaya.

CHAFFEE. Well, she ain't much, but I guess she'll do. Corporal, get the place ready for the Major. Dust it off a bit.

HANLEY. Yes sir. *(Hanley and Maridol start removing dust cloths from the furniture. Chaffee goes over to the pitcher of water, pours some out in the basin and washes his hands. Then he sits down heavily.)*

CHAFFEE. There he is — trying to defend himself in the bargain. Man's not even a lawyer.

HANLEY. No sir.

CHAFFEE. Watch out, Corporal. He won't be your easiest patient. *(Chaffee pours himself a glass of whiskey and knocks it back.)*

HANLEY. What exactly does he have, sir?

CHAFFEE. What doesn't he have? Malaria. Bonebreak Fever. The Bloody Flux ...

HANLEY. The Bloody Flux?

MARIDOL. *(Quietly.)* You all get it.

CHAFFEE. Don't ask too much of him, understand?

HANLEY. *(He doesn't.)* Yes ... Sir. *(Chaffee rises heavily.)*

9

CHAFFEE. Guard him like a prisoner — but treat him like a guest.

HANLEY. Yes sir! *(Confused.)* Don't you think he might try to escape?

CHAFFEE. Our Southern *Cavalier?* Not likely.

HANLEY. Oh.

CHAFFEE. Have him looking fit for tomorrow. I'm holding you personally responsible. *(Chaffee prepares to leave.)*

HANLEY. Sir! Aren't you gonna stay 'til he gets here?

CHAFFEE. No, you're in charge. *(Pause.)* Think you're up to it?

HANLEY. Yessir! I've seen me some action. *(Chaffee looks around one last time with concern.)*

CHAFFEE. She better make up a bed in this room. If that fever spikes again she should be on hand.

HANLEY. Yes sir. *(Chaffee starts to leave. Hanley comes to attention, salutes. Chaffee briskly returns the salute and exits. Hanley looks around the room.)* Well, I'm sure I don't know where he expects *you* to sleep. The Major gets the bed.

MARIDOL. I brought my mat. I'll put it down here. *(She points to the corner stage left.)*

HANLEY. *(Pointing toward the door.)* I got an extra camp bed out —

MARIDOL. I prefer my mat.

HANLEY. Fair enough. *(Maridol exits stage left and soon returns, with a rolled-up straw sleeping mat and a satchel, a large handwoven square of cloth with the corners tied. She leaves the mat rolled up against the wall. She continues to dust and tidy up the room. Hanley closes the shutters. Then, distracted, he goes over to the shelf and discovers a pile of old newspapers.)*

MARIDOL. No one has been here for a while.

HANLEY. Would ya look at this! *The San Francisco Chronicle* — only four weeks old! *(Hanley takes off his holster and pistol and slings it over the chair. He then sits down at the table and starts to read.)*

MARIDOL. *(Concentrating on her work.)* Ala-ee. It is very dusty. *(She dusts the shelf, taking the opportunity to pick up and examine each bottle carefully before dusting it and putting it in place. She picks up a bottle of quinine and looks at it, then the others, with surprise.)*

HANLEY. Hey, careful with that! *(She startles, almost guiltily, and puts the bottle back.)*

MARIDOL. Quinine! Where did you get this?

HANLEY. They left it for the Major.

MARIDOL. We ran out of it at the hospital.

HANLEY. *(Absorbed in the paper.)* Look here! They started up a new baseball team. The "Cleveland Indians." *(He grins.)* — 'bout the only Injuns left around there! *(He turns a page, then reads aloud.)* This one's about the Philippines. *(With some difficulty.)* "Congressional testi-mony resumed yesterday regarding alle-ga-tions of miscon-duct in Ba-batangas … "

MARIDOL. *(With quiet intensity.)* Batangas. [Bah TAHNG gahss] It is a province. *(Beat.)* To the south.

HANLEY. *(Lying.)* I knew that! *(He shrugs it off, and turns the page.)*

MARIDOL. *(In a flat voice.)* You did.

HANLEY. Well, too many five-dollar words, anyhow. *(Pause. Then, disappointed.)* But nothin' about the trial … *(He looks at the paper.)* Lordy. You got the Chinese fightin' the foreigners in Shanghai … And the British with the … Bo-ers in South Africa. *(With satisfaction.)* Little wars bustin' out all over! *(He grins up at Maridol, then approaches to the map on the wall.)* I just wish I knew which side we're supposed to be on …

MARIDOL. With the British. Aren't British and Americans the same?

HANLEY. Hell no! We fought them for independence! Don't you know yer history?

MARIDOL. *(With no affect.)* Oh. *(She continues to clean and unpack. She places her cloth satchel on the ground, unties the corners and removes some objects carefully. She extracts a Madonna and looks for a spot to put her. Hanley looks at her in alarm.)*

HANLEY. Just what do you think you're doin'?

MARIDOL. I have a name.

HANLEY. That's as may be, but I already forgot it.

MARIDOL. *(Quickly and frostily.)* Maridol Amaya.

HANLEY. That one word or two?

MARIDOL. Maridol. Call me Maridol. *(Pause.)* And what am I to call you? Corporal?

HANLEY. Corporal John Hanley. *(Beat.)* But Hanley'll do. *(Pause.)* So, Mary Dole, just what do you think you are doing there?

MARIDOL. *(Glancing down to the figure, speaking simply.)* I cannot do my work without Our Lady.

HANLEY. So they haven't converted you yet?

MARIDOL. Converted? To what?

HANLEY. Christianity.

MARIDOL. *(Indignantly.)* I am a good Catholic.

HANLEY. That's what I mean. Back home we say a Papists' as good as a Jew.

11

MARIDOL. *(Genuinely puzzled.)* I do not know … I have never met a Jew. *(Pause and a curious look.)* Have you?

HANLEY. *(Reluctantly.)* Well, no. *(Beat.)* But do not fear. Our missionaries are on their way.

MARIDOL. Corporal Hanley, I could go back the hospital now.

HANLEY. *(Hiding his panic.)* No need for that. But — what if Major Waller is offended by that *idol* in his room?

MARIDOL. *(Mildly.)* I only know that when I care for the sick, I ask for her help. *(She puts the Madonna on the shelf and strokes its base as though to reassure it. Then she turns back to him.)*

HANLEY. *(Looking around nervously.)* Just don't light the candles, OK?

MARIDOL. *(Serenely.)* Not until my prayers. *(She takes out a second figurine and puts it on a lower shelf.)*

HANLEY. Wait! What's that?

MARIDOL. Quan Yin. [Kwan Yinn] The Chinese Goddess of Mercy.

HANLEY. *(Groaning.)* So you *are* a heathen.

MARIDOL. I used to work for a Chinese doctor on Kipuya [Kih POO ya] Street. He taught me many useful things. Our Lady assists me. *(Beat.)* And Quan Yin assists her. *(She smiles happily.)* I think they are friends.

HANLEY. Now that's just ridiculous.

MARIDOL. Oh no. Not at all. Quan Yin is the patroness of women and sailors. *(Beat.)* And people under arrest.

HANLEY. *(Struggling to keep up.)* What?

MARIDOL. So we should make her feel welcome! *(She goes to her bag and gets out some sewing. Hanley, with the newspaper still open before him, looks at her in consternation. She smiles at him and — intentionally? — pronounces his name as though it's Chinese.)* So, Han Li, you consider yourself a Christian?

HANLEY. I certainly do.

MARIDOL. Please explain to me, which tribe do you belong to? Are you Pres-bee-tee-rian like Doctor Miller?

HANLEY. Oh no, they're not tribes. They're *denominations.* And we're Church of Christ.

MARIDOL. *(She brightens.)* Oh, but so are we!

HANLEY. No, we're *The* Church of Christ.

MARIDOL. So … you mean that we are not? *(She shakes her head.)* This is all curious to me. In the hospital, I have taken care of so many soldiers. Mett-o-dists, Bap-tists, Loot-er-ans. Poor

Private Flannigan, he used to say he was a Catholic like me. *(Pause. She considers.)* But he was not like me.

HANLEY. I should say not. *(She returns to her sewing, then peers back at him.)*

MARIDOL. But he was also not like you. He was from Ireland. *(Pause.)* You're not from Ireland.

HANLEY. No. I'm from Oklahoma Territory.

MARIDOL. *(Taking it in.)* And that is not Ireland.

HANLEY. No, Ma'am. That is not Ireland.

MARIDOL. So it is a State.

HANLEY. Nooooooo … It's a Territory.

MARIDOL. *(She purses her lips, then looks at him sideways.)* You Americans are *very* complicated. Some of you are from Ireland, which is not United States. But you, you are from United States Not-a-State.

HANLEY. Now hold on a —

MARIDOL. — and the way you talk. First you ask for my help. Then you shout at me and say "Chop chop." *(Pause.)* What does this mean — "Chop chop"?

HANLEY. *(Abashed.)* I didn't mean — [anything by it]

MARIDOL. Do you think it is Tagalog? [Tah GAH log] I do not think it is any language. "Chop chop." *(Pause.)* And now you say to me — "Ma'am." Which I believe for you is a title of respect.

HANLEY. I guess … it's from hearing you talk about our men. It makes you a little less … strange. Like you welcome us here.

MARIDOL. Perhaps I am here for the payment. Perhaps I do not like any creature to suffer. *(Pause. She stands and looks at him dangerously.)* Or perhaps I am an *insurrecto* spy!

HANLEY. *(He starts to rise.)* Now hold on a minute … *(Maridol laughs. He is embarrassed at falling for it:)* Oh, go on. *(Maridol is still laughing, but then her eyes fix on his face. She stops laughing and studies him closely.)*

MARIDOL. You are sick too. Your eyes — they're yellow. You've got the fever.

HANLEY. *(Shrugging it off.)* Had it. Back in Cuba. But now I'm ready to see some action!

MARIDOL. *(She winces slightly, then returns to her sewing.)* I will make a tea from the ginger root that will help you. *(She starts to rise.)*

LIEUTENANT. *(Offstage; faintly.)* Detail, halt. Right face. *(Hanley looks towards the window and jumps up.)*

HANLEY. You wait here. *(He starts for the door, then turns back.)*

And don't speak 'less you're spoken to! *(Hanley runs out the door, dashes back in, grabs his hat and plants it on his head, then runs out again. The following lines are heard only faintly.)*

LIEUTENANT. *(Offstage, muffled.)* Corporal, we are now placing the prisoner in your charge.

HANLEY. *(Offstage, almost inaudible.)* That's right, sir, just up that way. *(Littleton Waller enters. Waller is exhausted but maintains a military bearing. He carries an officer's valise. He walks over to the table.)*

LIEUTENANT. *(Offstage.)* Detail, left face. Forward, march. *(Maridol quickly and quietly places her sewing on the table and stands, eyes downcast. Waller does not take this in. He puts down his valise and dully looks around him. The only thing he fully notes is that this does not seem to be a prison. He squints, then rubs his eyes. Yet for all his ailments, he is still a man who commands instant authority. Hanley enters. He stands at attention and salutes the Marine Major. Waller does not return the salute. A long beat.)*

WALLER. *(With weary disparagement.)* What do you think you're doing?

HANLEY. *(Flustered.)* I'm waiting for the Major to return my salute. *(Beat.)* Sir.

WALLER. You one of those army boys that likes to salute indoors?

HANLEY. Yes sir. *(Glancing towards his pistol.)* When we're under arms. *(Long nervous beat.)* Sir.

WALLER. *(Shaking his head.)* Well, we can remedy that. *(Waller steps over to withdraw Hanley's pistol from the holster hung over the chair. Hanley starts to protest. Waller shoots him a look and Hanley falls back into position — withdraws his salute, looks to his side, then snaps to attention. Waller waves the pistol towards Hanley's hat.)*

HANLEY. What?

WALLER. Your cover! *(Hanley whips off his hat, places it under his left arm, and returns to attention.)*

HANLEY. Sir!

WALLER. *(Sighs.)* That's better. *(Waller places the pistol as far out of reach as possible on the shelf and turns back to Hanley. Waller makes a sound of relief.)* Now we can both feel safer. *(Waller lapses back into himself, while Hanley stands, ignored, at attention with increasing discomfort. Long, long pause. Hanley catches Maridol's eye, she shrugs. Finally Waller notices him.)* At ease. *(Hanley is finally at ease. Waller squints at him.)* Are you new?

HANLEY. No-o-o-o. *(Long beat.)* Sir. *(Waller disregards him. Waller sits down heavily in a chair at the table and looks around the room.)*

WALLER. It was decent of Chaffee to afford me this courtesy. I can see this was the home of an aristocrat. *(Maridol looks around the room with a sense of familiarity. Waller leans back and closes his eyes. Maridol takes the opportunity to snatch her sewing from the table. Waller half opens his eyes and looks at her foggily.)*

MARIDOL. *(Caught.)* I am sorry.

WALLER. *(Confused.)* What? *(Pause.)* Oh. No need to … worry … on my account. *(Waller closes his eyes.)*

HANLEY. Do you … need anything, Major? *(Waller opens his eyes.)*

WALLER. *(Foggily.)* I only … wish to know my circumstances.

HANLEY. What do you mean, sir? *(Waller raises his head and focuses unsteadily on Hanley and Maridol — as though he were staring into the sun. He is drunk with fatigue.)*

WALLER. *(Struggling to put it together.)* Last spring I was decorated for valor in China. Come winter I was in Samar, dying of fever. A few weeks ago we set sail for Manila — and they cheered us as we passed! *(Pause.)*

HANLEY. Yes sir.

WALLER. But yesterday — *(He squints.)* if memory serves — I seemed to be defending myself in an Army court martial. With an Army judge, and — *(He looks at Hanley skeptically.)* — what *passes* for an Army guard.

HANLEY. *(Offended.)* Sir!

WALLER. *(Ignoring him.)* So many reversals of fortune. *(Pause.)* So tell me, boy — who am I today?

HANLEY. *(Stiffly.)* You're a prisoner of the court, sir. Under … "exceptional" … circumstances.

WALLER. *(Smiles.)* "Exceptional"! *(Beat.)* That is how I surely feel — *exceptional.* *(Waller squints towards Hanley's insignia.)* — is it corporal?

HANLEY. Corporal Hanley, sir.

WALLER. *(Indicating Maridol.)* And she is…?

HANLEY. Oh, she's just a servan—

MARIDOL. — I am a nurse. I work for Captain Miller in the wards in Tondo. I was told that I am needed here. *(Hanley regards her resentfully.)*

WALLER. I see. *(To Hanley.)* Did General Chaffee give you any notion of when to expect the verdict? I'd like to prepare myself for — the occasion.

HANLEY. Tomorrow morning, Sir. *(Beat.)*

WALLER. *(He makes a sound of derision. He looks to the day bed,*

15

changes gear.) A bed with good linens, in a civilized room. With a pianoforte [Piano FOR tay] in the corner, I'd think I was in Virginia. *(Beat. He grins bitterly.)* Course, if I *was* in Virginia — I'd leave.

HANLEY. *(Long beat.)* Can I get you anything, sir?

WALLER. I wouldn't mind a glass of water. *(He looks at both of them acidly.)* That is, if it it's not poisoned.

HANLEY. This is Manila, sir. We make sure to boil it. *(Hanley nods to Maridol, who fetches the water. Waller gets up and goes to the window, opens the shutter, and looks out. Brutal sunlight floods into the room.)*

WALLER. *(Squinting painfully into the light.)* I can see the river from here. *(Turning to face them.)* That is the Pasig, [PAH sig] is it not? *(Pause.)*

HANLEY. I'm not right sure —

MARIDOL. It is.

WALLER. *(Not listening to them.)* I never did see a river run so brown, with such a stench. I swear, the motto must be, "If it's dead, throw it in the river." *(Maridol brings him a tall, cloudy glass of water, which he accepts and sips.)*

HANLEY. General Chaffee told me it contained a good deal of … brown matter, sir.

WALLER. Brown matter. Well, Chaffee should know.

HANLEY. Sir! The General is our commanding officer!

WALLER. *Your* commanding officer, army boy. That much gets him obedience. You have to *earn* respect. *(His face closes down.)* I'm tired, soldier.

MARIDOL. You should take your quinine, Major.

WALLER. God help me. Well, go ahead. *(Maridol gets the quinine and an eyedropper and puts two drops in the glass of water, which Waller now drinks with even greater disgust.)*

HANLEY. Would you like me to stay or to leave, sir?

WALLER. You might as well stay, corporal. Stop apologizing for the army and sit down.

HANLEY. *(He starts to protest, under his breath.)* I never did! *(Waller cuts him off with a wave, and squints again towards the bright light at the window.)*

WALLER. But close the shutters. *(Softer.)* Let it be Virginia.

HANLEY. *(Pause.)* Yes sir. *(Hanley closes the shutters and sits down with Waller at the table.)*

WALLER. I am not the best of company. The courtroom was … debilitating. *(Pause.)* We bring the rule of law unto the heathen — but we wield it so erratically ourselves.

HANLEY. Do you want me to unpack your bag, sir?

WALLER. That won't be necessary. Just move it out of the way. *(He gestures. Hanley moves the bag to the side of the room, but as he does so, his eyes catch on the monogram.)* What're you starin' at?

HANLEY. Well … I was just noticin' your monogram — LWTW. It's … unusual.

WALLER. Indeed it is. Littleton Waller Tazewell [TEZ well] Waller.

HANLEY. *(Not sure he heard it right.)* Littleton *Waller Tazewell* Waller? *(Hanley sits.)*

WALLER. That's right, son. A walking illustration of patrician inbreeding. And we Littletons, Wallers, Tazewells — and the — *(He waves a hand dismissively.) other* Wallers — have been inbreeding since 1654. *(Pause.)* You might say the blood is … *pure.*

HANLEY. Out in the Territory we're all mongrels — I wouldn't know a blue blood if I saw one.

WALLER. *(Sharply.)* I didn't say blue, son. It's Virginia. Our blood runs gray.

HANLEY. *(Beat.)* That's what was so fine about the Rough Riders, sir.

WALLER. Rough Riders?

HANLEY. Yes sir! There we were, city boys from the North and cowboys from the South, all pullin' together 'gainst the tyranny of Spain. Like we was all one country again.

WALLER. *(Remotely.)* Yes …

HANLEY. We joined up in San Antone and shipped out from Tampa Bay. And I'll tell you, when we rolled through Dixie, those people *cheered* for Old Glory! First time since the War of the Rebellion —

WALLER. *(He cuts him off sharply.)* — The War of Northern Aggression! *(Skeptically interested.)* Yes, that may be. But tell me, son, who led your charge?

HANLEY. What do you mean, sir?

WALLER. For your blessed "Volunteers." A cowboy like you? Or perhaps a gallant Southern officer?

HANLEY. Why no sir, neither. We fought under Colonel Roosevelt. [ROO se velt]

WALLER. And that is my point. *(Beat.)* A loud little man with a Harvard degree. Only uniform he ever wore was one he bought himself — at Abercrombie and Fitch!

HANLEY. It — got pretty rough, sir.

WALLER. I'm sure it did. You run up the hill and sang "I'm the king of the castle" and got your picture taken for mama and the hometown news. That's war for you. Ain't it grand.

HANLEY. You mean it's different here. Sir.

WALLER. It is. *(Silence.)*

MARIDOL. Major, you should rest. *(Waller rebels, gets up and paces with a stubborn new energy. He walks up to the campaign map and looks at it intently. He traces a route on it in Samar, then turns back to them.)*

WALLER. These must have been officer's quarters. *(Pause. He turns sharply back to them.)* Haven't you any amusements?

HANLEY. *(Taking playing cards from his breast pocket.)* I got a deck a cards.

WALLER. No!

HANLEY. *(Taken aback; looking around.)* There might be something. *(They look around.)*

WALLER. *(Pointing.)* A chess set. Splendid! *(Hanley bring the chess set over to the table and hands it to Waller, who places it down carefully. The pieces are already set up on the board. Hanley sits.)* The game of cardinals and kings ... *(He holds up and examines one of the pieces.)* This one's uncommonly fine. Onyx and bone? I saw sets like this in China. *(He turns to Maridol.)* Young woman! Come here.

MARIDOL. Yes. *(She comes over.)*

WALLER. Sit down, just sit down right here. *(She sits at the table and watches impassively.)* I'd like to give you a glimpse of civilization.

HANLEY. Your very first.

MARIDOL. Oh?

WALLER. *(Heedless.)* Look at these pieces lined up on the board, all clean-scrubbed and prime[d] for glory. *(Beat.)* All right corporal, *now* we can pass the evening.

HANLEY. I can't say ... as I know how to play.

WALLER. Oh, now that *is* a damned shame.

HANLEY. I play checkers. Isn't it about the same?

WALLER. No-o-o, soldier. Not at all. *(He lovingly fingers the pieces as he talks.)* In checkers, all men are created equal — with an equal chance of getting crowned. *(He smiles.)* Or — slain. *(Beat.)* Such a lovely dream. *(Pause.)* But in *chess* ... every piece has its own birthright. A pawn does not aspire to be king — he exists to hold his territory. *(He looks up suddenly.)*

HANLEY. I see ...

WALLER. Do you know who gave us the game of chess, soldier?

HANLEY. The British?

WALLER. No sir! The A-rabs. Master strategists. *(Hanley picks up*

a chess piece and studies it.)
HANLEY. I hear it's pretty hard.
WALLER. It's all about learning the rules, boy. That's the test of civilized combat. Know the true character of every piece. *(Heating up.)* The pawns are brave little fellows, but of limited imagination. A step or two forward, an attack to the side. *(He gestures diagonally.)* The king has more options, but he's not so brave. Spends his time lurking at the rear. *(Waller studies the board and moves the pieces as he names them, setting them into formation.)*
HANLEY. Like a war.
WALLER. No, soldier. Too obvious. *(Beat.)* Why not call it a courtroom. Now let's see … the pawns can be the jury. Some Army, some Marines — Why mercy! the Marines appear to be outnumbered. Now how did *that* happen?
HANLEY. What, sir?
WALLER. Let's line 'em up and paint a righteous expression on their blank little faces. *(Conspiratorial whisper.)* "The Major had some prisoners shot! Oh dearie dearie me!" Look at 'em! It could have been any one of them up in the dock instead.
HANLEY. What do you mean?
WALLER. *(Holding up the black knight.)* And the army prosecutor, with his sideways leaps of logic. "Did Major Waller give the orders? Or did Major Waller follow orders?"
MARIDOL. Major, you should not excite yourself! *(Waller jumps up and points at the chessboard jury, erupting.)*
HANLEY. What orders?
MARIDOL. *(Trying to quiet him.)* Corporal!
WALLER. *(Waller stares angrily at the board.)* We shouldn't even be here!
HANLEY. *(Looking at the chessboard.)* Where?
WALLER. An Army court has no jurisdiction over a Marine! *(He sits down deflated. There is a pause. Distantly.)* But we — will not speak of the trial.
HANLEY. What orders?
MARIDOL. *(To Hanley, shushing again.)* Please! *(A long, unnerving pause. Hanley looks from Waller to Maridol, feeling he should do something.)*
HANLEY. Major? *(Beat.)* Major? *(Hanley turns to Maridol.)* What should we do?
MARIDOL. *(Coldly.)* You are asking me?
HANLEY. Yes!

MARIDOL. The "servant"?

HANLEY. I'm sorry! *(Maridol chews on this. Then she walks over to Waller and regards him with a kind but professional eye.)*

MARIDOL. I think he must eat.

HANLEY. Major? Have you eaten today? *(Waller is silent.)*

MARIDOL. *(Gently.)* Would you like some ... food? *(Waller stares ahead — not exactly answering, he's describing his tumultuous gut.)*

WALLER. Food is not ... agreeable ... to me ... at this time.

MARIDOL. So not food. *(Beat.)* I will give you rice soup. For invalids.

WALLER. *(Half-stirring, distant.)* Ah yes ... nursery food ...

HANLEY. Well fine then! Make it!

MARIDOL. *(Turning to him coolly.)* "Makiraan." [MAH kee rah AHN]

HANLEY. What?

WALLER. *(Distantly.)* "Please." *(Beat.)* It means — "Please."

HANLEY. *(Back to her, tersely.)* Please.

MARIDOL. Oo oo. [OH oh] *(Hanley stares. Beat. Maridol exits. Waller continues to sit woodenly in the chair. Hanley approaches him, coaxingly.)*

HANLEY. Maybe you'd like to sit by the window. We might get an evening breeze. *(Waller starts to rouse himself. His stomach hurts.)*

WALLER. It's that damn quinine — it's hell on the gut.

MARIDOL. You are lucky to have it.

HANLEY. For malaria?

WALLER. I can't seem to shake it. Samar, Leyte, [LAY tay] Luzon — the whole damn country's riddled with it.

HANLEY. Luzon. I've been there.

WALLER. Indeed? And do you know where you are now?

HANLEY. Of course, sir! In Manila.

WALLER. *(Smiling.)* Of course. Show me. On the map. *(Waller walks over to the map on the wall. Hanley lopes over to the map, puts up a finger, but quickly becomes confused.)*

HANLEY. *(Tracing with his finger.)* Manila ... Manila ... *(Beat.)* All right. Here yonder is China, so you go due east and ... then ... you ... *(A pause, scanning it with consternation.)* I know ... it's around here somewhere ...

WALLER. Look. *(He points.)* Manila's the city. Luzon's *(He makes a big circle.)* the island. Manila is in Luzon. *(Beat.)* Don't worry, son, most of the folks back in Washington can't find it either.

HANLEY. *(Scanning the islands.)* There's just so many of them.

20

WALLER. *(Laughing at him.)* That's right, soldier. The Philippines — seven thousand islands, scattered across a rocky sea. *(He looks at the map calculatingly.)* It's not properly a place at all, you know. That Magellan? He sailed past some islands and made him a map. Then he drew a big circle 'round 'em to claim 'em for the king of Spain. Old Philip. One stroke of the pen — and *(He snaps his fingers.)* all those tribes, who had nothing in common, suddenly became Philip —

HANLEY. *(Overlapping.)* — lipinos!

WALLER. Must a come as quite a shock. Once they found out ... *(Maridol enters with a wooden tray containing a bowl of soup and a spoon. She puts the tray down on the table quietly and observes them.)* And now we own the whole damn shootin' match.

HANLEY. I was never quite clear on that, sir.

WALLER. Don't you read the papers?

MARIDOL. *(Under her breath.)* Not the big words ... *(Hanley shoots her a look to shut up.)*

WALLER. Well. Once we whupped the Spaniards, our dear departed President thought we should hold on to Manila, as a fueling station ... But one night, as he lay sleeping, God himself paid a visit. *(They consider this.)* And God said: "William — not just Manila. I want you to take them all. And why don't you — civilize 'em for me ... "

HANLEY. *(Also uncertain.)* Well *that* was lucky. *(Maridol is not happy.)*

WALLER. So we bought them off Spain for twenty million dollars, and now they're ours. *(Long beat.)* Must a come as quite a shock ...

HANLEY. Twenty million dollars? For seven thousand islands?

WALLER. That's right.

HANLEY. That's just ... *(Rapidly.)* twenny eight hunnerd and fifty-seven dollars per island!

WALLER. Where'd you get that?

HANLEY. I got a gift for mental arithmetic.

WALLER. I should say so.

HANLEY. And how many folks?

WALLER. Population? ... oh, round eight million.

HANLEY. Damn! That's but two-bucks fifty a head! *(Maridol slams a bowl on the table.)*

MARIDOL. Here! *(She exits angrily.)*

WALLER. Son.

HANLEY. Yes sir? *(Waller glances towards the door where Maridol exited.)*

WALLER. *(Sotto voce.)* We don't talk that way any more.

HANLEY. No sir. *(Hanley looks back at the map.)* So where are we now?

WALLER. Look here. Think of the whole archipelago *(His hand sweeps down across the curve of the islands.)* as a giant cobra. Up here — Luzon [LOO zon] — the flaring head, ready to strike. That's where the war started. Last year we pushed the insurgents south to *(He flattens his hand and pushes south.)* Batangas.

HANLEY. I hear it's pretty ugly down there. Can't wait to ship out!

WALLER. *(Thrown.)* Ship out? Oh, yes. *(Long beat. Then abruptly resuming.)* The Batangans have always been rebels, even under the Spaniards. So Chaffee's takin' a page outa General Sheridan's book — from the Virginia Campaign.

HANLEY. How's that?

WALLER. Burn 'em out. Shoot the men and boys. Then herd the women and children into camps. Malaria takes care of *them.* *(Pause.)*

HANLEY. Does it work? *(Long beat; Waller's lost in thought.)* Major?

WALLER. *(He's remembering something. Pause.)* Does it work? *(Long pause. Then he turns abruptly back to the map.)* And here, you have the long sharp spine curving into the sea. That's Samar. [SA mar]

HANLEY. Where you were.

WALLER. Where I was.

HANLEY. They're still fighting?

WALLER. *(He affirms. Then, more rapidly.)* And now we move south, to the cobra's tail. Mindanao. *(He points to the southern islands. Maridol enters, bringing a serving dish of soup, and places it on the table.)* The sting in the tail! You see, soldier, those islands are Muslim, and they are fierce. They didn't like the Spaniards and they don't like us. They hate the Tagalogs — *(Pause.)* Hell, they don't even like each other!

MARIDOL. They are savages. *(The men ignore her.)*

WALLER. We haven't even gotten to *them* ...

HANLEY. *(Fervently.)* But we will, sir, we will. We will storm ashore —

WALLER. Corporal — [you can't just say that]

HANLEY. *(Pointing to the map.)* — Say! Lookee here — the tip of the tail — "Zamboanga." Like the song ...

WALLER. What?

22

HANLEY. *(Starting in with the last two lines, picking up speed.)*
    Oh the monkeys have no tails, they were bitten off by whales,
    Oh the monkeys have no tails in Zamboanga.
(See Appendix for song.)
MARIDOL. *(Overlapping, puzzled.)* Monkeys with no tails? I do not know these monkeys.
HANLEY. *(Laughing.)* For Pete's sake, they're not talking about monkeys! They're —
WALLER. — Soldier!
HANLEY. *(Sobering rapidly.)* Yes sir?
WALLER. *(Pointing.)* Your mouth.
HANLEY. What?
WALLER. Shut it. *(Hanley's mouth hangs open for a moment. He closes it. Maridol sits.)*
HANLEY. *(To Waller:)* You know, for the longest time … I didn't even know that Zamboanga was a real place.
WALLER. *(Distantly.)* It's not. I've been there … Nothing real about it …
MARIDOL. Major Waller, your soup is ready.
WALLER. I thank you. Why I've almost got me an appetite. *(He looks at the table and sees only one place setting.)* Corporal, aren't you going to dine?
HANLEY. I had this figured for an officer's mess, sir. I was planning to eat outside.
WALLER. I appreciate your sentiments, corporal. But given the *paucity* of other officers *(He looks around jokingly.)*, I invite you to join me. *(Pause.)* Three weeks of detention has lowered my standards. *(Hanley sits down.)*
MARIDOL. *(Formally, to Hanley.)* Do you want some rice soup?
HANLEY. I don' know, I'm pretty hungry … What else is there?
MARIDOL. They left some Army beef and biscuits.
HANLEY. Embalmed meat? No thanks! I'd sooner eat that newspaper!
MARIDOL. That is all there is. Except for rice soup … and what I am having.
HANLEY. Then I want some of that.
MARIDOL. No you do not.
HANLEY. Well I sure do. *(Waller stifles a laugh.)*
MARIDOL. Corporal Hanley, you do not want to eat what I eat.
HANLEY. I don't see why not! *(Pause.)* What is it?
MARIDOL. *Pancit* [Pahn SEET] and *baluut* [Bah LOOT].

23

HANLEY. Well … What's that?

MARIDOL. Fried noodles and boiled egg.

HANLEY. Why didn't you say so? Serve it right up! *(Waller sputters into his soup.)* You all right, sir?

WALLER. *(Stifling a laugh.)* Fine, soldier, fine. *(Pause.)* Sure you don't want some rice soup?

HANLEY. No sir! I've got me an appetite. *(Maridol stalks out the door. There's a pause. Waller suddenly looks at Hanley intently.)*

WALLER. *(Strangely.)* You're very like him.

HANLEY. Sir?

WALLER. Billy Perkins. That red-headed boy from Kansas. Served under me in the China campaign.

HANLEY. But I'm from the Territory, sir.

WALLER. I taught Perkins how to play poker one night in Peking. Damn near cleaned me out. He had real talent.

HANLEY. I favor blackjack myself, sir.

WALLER. He was soakin' up everything I knew. Wanted to be an officer.

HANLEY. Me too! I've got "potential."

WALLER. *(Beat.)* And he shared your simple-minded optimism …

HANLEY. Sir?

WALLER. He was killed you know. *(His face closes off.)* The Ninth Infantry massacre. In Samar last September. *(Puzzled, starting to see the burial ground.)* There were so many … I don't know why that red-haired boy should stick in my mind.

HANLEY. You were there?

WALLER. No. I saw them off from Subic Bay. Gave Perkins a brand new deck a cards … *(Maridol walks back in with a graceful little stomp. Now she carries two plates of fried noodles each with a large egg and fork. She sets one of them sharply on the table in front of Hanley.)*

MARIDOL. Here. *(She retreats to her corner and begins to eat.)*

HANLEY. Well, this is fine. A whole lot better than Army chow! Hell, some men died from the rations back in Cuba!

WALLER. I'm partial to Cuban food myself. *Moros y cristianos.*

HANLEY. You were in Cuba?

WALLER. Battle of Santiago Bay …

HANLEY. So there *we* were, with ol' Teddy, steamin' past Guantánamo. And *you* were but a few miles out to sea.

WALLER. *(Looking into the distance.)* We had the Spanish fleet trapped in the harbor, square in our gunsights. Their honor depended on sneaking past and ours depended on knocking 'em

24

out. So down they went, one by one, like a sorry game of marbles ...

HANLEY. We did the right thing there, sir. Those Spaniards, they blew up our ship.

WALLER. The Maine? — that's not certain. But they surely did misuse the Cubans. We could not tolerate such behavior on our doorstep. *(He looks around.)* I'm just not sure why we're *here* ... *(Waller looks to Maridol with curiosity.)* What about you, young lady? Any words of kindness for the Spaniards?

MARIDOL. No, sir. *(Beat.)* They killed my father. *(Waller regards her briefly with curiosity, which she ignores.)*

WALLER. And why was that?

MARIDOL. He fought for independence. So they shot him in the plaza.

WALLER. *(Sympathetic and impressed.)* ... a Secessionist ... *(Beat.)* I am sorry. *(To Hanley.)* How's your meal, soldier? Better than hardtack?

HANLEY. Yes sir! These noodles aren't half bad. Little bits of pork, and cabbage, and ... *(He looks down at his plate.)* ... thangs ... mixed in.

WALLER. And how's the egg?

HANLEY. *(He shrugs.)* An egg's an egg, sir.

WALLER. *(Amused.)* Is that so?

HANLEY. Well sure. *(Hanley picks it up and peels the shell off. He holds the peeled egg over the plate in his other hand and bites into it. Waller and Maridol watch him with great interest. Suddenly Hanley drops the egg and the plate, which breaks. He stands up and explodes, his mouth sputtering bits of egg onto the table. Angrily:)* What in tarnation? *(He reaches into his mouth and pulls out small bones. Waller starts to laugh. Hanley looks from Waller to Maridol, in accusatory disbelief.)* It crunched! There's a ... baby duck ... in there! *(He reaches into his mouth again and pulls a long, wet, yellow feather. Waller continues to laugh, and Maridol looks grimly satisfied.)*

WALLER. *(Laughing at him.)* Eggs with legs!

HANLEY. *(To Maridol.)* You ... you...!

WALLER. Don't blame the girl, soldier — you asked for *baluut!* [Bah-LOOT]

MARIDOL. *(With supreme indifference.)* You eat the bird. You eat the egg. *We* eat them together. I do not see the difference. *(She rises with all deliberation, crosses to the table, picks up the rest of his egg from the plate and eats it ostentatiously. There is an audible "crunch crunch crunch." Then she neatly brushes the broken crockery into a cloth and returns to her seat.)*

25

WALLER. *(Shaking his head mournfully.)* Pore little ducky …
HANLEY. *(Alarmed.)* There's just one thing I need to know —
WALLER. What's that, soldier?
HANLEY. *(In a panicked whisper.)* What were those *thangs* in the noodles? *(Lights out.)*

Scene 2

A Valiant Attempt to Sleep

Lights up. The shutters are open again, and the light is now softer, going towards evening. Over this scene, the lights change, very gradually, from fading daylight to light cobalt evening blue. Maridol's chair is now by the window. The table has been cleared. Waller's jacket is hung on the back of his chair. He is reclined on the bed and seems to be sleeping. Hanley sits at the table, pretending to read the newspaper spread out before him. Throughout the scene they speak in audible voices, but ones that suggest they don't want to wake the Major. Maridol is bending over Waller. She stands up and addresses Hanley.

MARIDOL. It's good he can sleep. *(There is a pause. She goes to her chair by the window and picks up her sewing.)*
HANLEY. *(To Maridol without looking at her.)* That was pretty rum, makin' a fool of me like that before the Major.
MARIDOL. *(Also not looking up.)* A fool makes himself. *(Pause.)* I did not offer you the egg. You demanded it.
HANLEY. How was I to know your pagan ways? *(There is silence.)*
MARIDOL. No one invited you here in the first place.
HANLEY. Invited? We came to free you from the Spaniards!
MARIDOL. *(She looks up at him.)* The Spaniards are gone, di-ba?
HANLEY. There's still fightin' in the south. See? Says so right here. *(He indicates newspaper.)* We need to finish the job.
MARIDOL. *(Nodding toward paper.)* Those are not Spaniards. They are Pilipinos.
HANLEY. Huh! *(Pause.)* Well, I surely won't fall for your egg trick again. Matter a fact, you ever set foot in Oklahoma, I'll get you back.

MARIDOL. *(Laughing.)* Me! In Oklahoma! That is a very funny idea.
HANLEY. Well I don't see why. No funnier than me being here. All you do is get on a boat. *(Pause.)* And then a train. *(Long pause.)* And then a horse. And there you are!
MARIDOL. *(She puts down her sewing and looks at him curiously.)* All right, corporal, your Oklahoma. Tell me what it is like.
HANLEY. *(Uncertain.)* Well, *everybody* knows what it's like. It's just … normal. You know, farms and ranches. And then you got your houses and stores — like a real town.
MARIDOL. Ah. *(Pause.)* And where is the plaza?
HANLEY. No plaza. More of a Main Street.
MARIDOL. *(Trying hard to imagine it.)* So where is your market?
HANLEY. You got the General Store. On Main Street. Not an open air market like here.
MARIDOL. *(Amazed.)* So everyone buys their coconuts from the same man!
HANLEY. Well, actually … we don't have coconuts.
MARIDOL. *(Pursing her lips.)* Now you are fooling *me*. *(With certainty.)* It is impossible to live without coconuts.
HANLEY. No, honest! We don't have any coconuts. *(She is briefly dumfounded, then stricken.)*
MARIDOL. I am so sorry! *(A pause as it sinks in.)* But how can you survive? No *palms* for your rooftops? No shells to make bowls? No sweet meat for your rice, no milk for the children!
HANLEY. *(Surprised at her distress.)* Hey … it's all right.
MARIDOL. *(Shaking her head sadly.)* No. I am feeling ashamed. I always thought you Americans came to the Philippines for plunder. But now I think you need our help. *(Maridol puts down her sewing, and goes to her bundle in the corner. She gets something out, and gives it to Hanley. We hear the clinking of small coins.)* Here. *Limós.* [Lee-MOSE] For the children. *(She goes back to her chair and picks up her sewing.)*
HANLEY. *(Pause.)* Keep your money! *(He returns the coins to her. Maridol responds mildly. She goes on sewing, then looks up at him suddenly.)*
MARIDOL. Corporal … I would like to ask you. What is the difference between a state and a territory?
HANLEY. Well, a territory's a place that's on the way to being a state. See, we got these natives called the Five Civilized Tribes, and we moved 'em into the territories so they could live peaceful. *(Pause.)* But then they found oil. So we had a Land Run so the rest

of us could have a shot at it. *(He pauses, a little confused himself.)*

MARIDOL. *(Shaking her head.)* You already told me you don't have tribes, you have denominations. *(Beat.)* You mean the Five Civilized *Denominations*.

HANLEY. No! There aren't Five Civilized Denominations!

MARIDOL. Well, there must be at least four! *(Beat.)*

HANLEY. *(Shaking his head.)* No! I mean —

MARIDOL. — and how did they decide what land would be in your Territory? Is it an island?

HANLEY. Not hardly. *(Pause. He's drawing a mental map.)* There's the Red River to the south. And Kansas up north.

MARIDOL. And in between?

HANLEY. *(Shrugging.)* A whole lot a red dirt.

MARIDOL. But why?

HANLEY. Darned if I know. *(Beat.)* Guess some fellow sat down and drew 'imself a circle.

WALLER. *(He's been listening, though not obviously.)* Or rather, a very deep fry pan. *(Waller sits up in the bed.)*

HANLEY. How are you feeling, Major?

WALLER. *(Waller rubs his head.)* Corporal, I'd like to say the sleep has done me good. *(Beat.)* But I cannot. *(Beat. He looks around.)* Give me a book — perhaps I can read. *(Hanley goes over to the shelf and grabs a book at random and brings it to Waller.)*

HANLEY. Uh, here, sir. *(Waller opens the book and begins to read, then throws it back to Hanley.)*

WALLER. I'm not going to read a dictionary.

HANLEY. Oh, sorry … *(He puts it on the table near Maridol, who regards it with great interest.)*

WALLER. *(Eyes closed, gesturing.)* There. In my bag. *(Hanley retrieves a book from Waller's valise and brings it over to him.)*

HANLEY. *(Looking at the spine.)* Don't see how you can read this, Major.

WALLER. *(Taking it.)* It's ancient history, corporal. Xenophon. *(ZEN o fon.)* He's been traveling with me since I was a boy. *(Beat.)* Surely you know Xenophon.

HANLEY. Can't say that I do.

WALLER. A Greek general, four centuries before Christ. He led an invasion of Persia.

HANLEY. *(Entranced.)* Persia!

WALLER. But his troops suffered a terrible defeat, and he was obliged to lead an [h]eroic retreat:

HANLEY. How can you have a heroic retreat?

WALLER. *(With growing excitement.)* Up the Tigris River. Over scorching deserts and treacherous cliffs, past hostile tribes and savage Kurds!

HANLEY. And then what happened?

WALLER. Xenophon and his men were perishing of hunger and thirst. They thought all was lost … and then …

HANLEY. *What? (Waller opens the book to a marked spot, looks down, and reads in a magical voice.)*

WALLER. "The Greeks catch sight of the sea."

HANLEY. He saved them!

WALLER. *(Long pause.)* I read this passage over and over … *(He leans back, then opens his eyes.)*

HANLEY. How did he do it?

WALLER. Ah! You see, corporal, every time the savages came up with a new trick, Xenophon outwitted them. He knew his adversary …

HANLEY. And then what? Did they crown him a king? And cover 'im with glory?

WALLER. No. *(Darkly.)* Once they got back there was nothing but blame. Xenophon was tried and sent into exile. *(Crestfallen beat.)*

HANLEY. Well that's a sorry story! *(A silence.)*

WALLER. You want to learn about strategy, son?

HANLEY. Yes sir!

WALLER. Well, you can start with the lesson of Xenophon: A good officer looks out for his men.

HANLEY. Oh … Yes sir. Is that all? *(Waller puts the book aside and leans back with his eyes closed.)*

WALLER. Is that all? *(He falls silent and tries to read.)*

HANLEY. You want me to open the shutters, get you some air?

WALLER. *(Tonelessly.)* As you wish … *(Hanley opens the shutters. The night is deepening. Hanley looks out into the night.)*

HANLEY. Well, one thing I'll say about this place. It's got nice weather. We've had sunshine for days.

WALLER. *(He puts the book aside and lies back, with his eyes closed.)* Corporal, I was wrong about you. You're not simple-minded. You're a buffoon.

HANLEY. What do you mean, sir?

WALLER. Haven't you ever heard of the rainy season? I suppose they don't have that in the Territory.

HANLEY. I never minded a little rain.

WALLER. And how do you feel about torrents? And your boots rotting offa your feet so you can march barefoot — through leech-infested waters?

HANLEY. Well, I — [didn't mean it like that.]

WALLER. — malaria! — and mudslides that bury a village in a heartbeat? That's what this benighted country is like for half the year! *(Beat.)* You just had the dumb luck to land in the other half.

HANLEY. Sorry.

WALLER. I shouldn't sleep any more. If I do, I'll be restless 'til morning. *(He looks at Hanley.)* I've got to be presentable tomorrow. *(He lies back on the bed and groans.)* God, I don't think I've slept in a year! *(Maridol goes to him and puts a hand on his forehead. He looks at her, a little disconcerted.)*

MARIDOL. *(To Hanley.)* It is the fever.

WALLER. Well, get rid of it, for God's sake. I won't have them sentence me as an invalid.

HANLEY. More quinine?

WALLER. No!

HANLEY. *(To Maridol.)* Can't you do something?

MARIDOL. *(To Waller.)* Do you want a cold compress?

WALLER. That would be fine. *(Maridol fetches a cloth and basin of water. She dampens and wrings the cloth out in the water and applies it across Waller's forehead.)*

MARIDOL. Here …

WALLER. You have a gentle touch.

MARIDOL. Does that feel better?

WALLER. My eyes are like to explode. *(Beat.)* It was hard … to stay … lucid … in court … with so many lies!

MARIDOL. You don't need to worry about it now …

WALLER. *(Dully.)* But at least I defended my honor. I wasn't about to plead guilty just to please the General. *(Waller sits up and looks at Hanley, seeing him and not seeing him.)*

WALLER. Hear that, corporal?

HANLEY. Hey, calm down Major, I'm not the jury.

MARIDOL. *(Firmly, with a look to Hanley.)* Major, you must not upset yourself. It will only make your head hurt more. *(Turning to Hanley.)* Corporal, talk to him. *(Beat. Sternly:)* Quietly.

WALLER. No, I don't want to hear that damn fool talk. You talk.

MARIDOL. Me? What can I talk about?

WALLER. I don't care. I like the sound of your voice. It soothes me. *(Pause.)* Speak to me of … Virginia.

MARIDOL. *(Looking at Hanley.)* But I don't know anything about —
HANLEY. *(Softly.)* — Virginia is his home. Just tell a pretty story.
MARIDOL. *(Gently, as to a child.)* Once there was a beautiful, beautiful island called — Virginia. *(She pronounces it "Vir-jee-nee-ah" throughout.)* And it was covered in lotus and wild orchids … and the people there were happy, and sang all the time. They loved to *(She thinks for a moment.)* … dive in the sea. For pearls. *(She steals a look at Waller. He is reclined, in a half-sitting position. He has closed his eyes and seems to have found some peace. He opens his eyes and looks at her mildly.)*
WALLER. Go on. What did the good folk of Virginia do with their pearls? *(He closes his eyes.)*
MARIDOL. They were most excellent pearls, these pearls of Virginia. Formed like tear-drops, pale blue-gray. *(She's getting lost in her story.)* These pearls came from shells shaped like small hands, that would open only in moonlight. *(She holds out her hands, pressed together one on top of the other. She opens the top palm slowly with a soft smile.)* The people of Virginia would find the shells by following the fish that swam over them. *(She continues to use her hands with small beautiful gestures.)* Blue fish, but not ordinary blue. A blue so clear that it trembled in the sun. Long fins, trailing in water … These fish thought they were guarding the shells. *(Now with sorrow.)* But they were only small fish, with no teeth. So instead of protecting the shells, they were really giving them away. *(She pauses, and looks at Waller, who is resting serenely.)* So the people of Virginia gathered up all the pearls and put them in their coconut — *(She looks, alarmed, to Hanley — are there coconuts in Virginia? He shrugs. A pause. She decides to go on.)* — shells. And took them home to string on a cord. The women wore necklaces on their feast days. And each man wore a pearl in his left ear. To show he was a true son of Virginia. *(She knows Waller is asleep again now. She checks on him, and smiles at Hanley.)* That is how it is. Is it not?
HANLEY. A hunnerd percent. *(Pause.)* Think he's asleep. *(He walks over to the window aimlessly. Maridol sits down at the table and returns to the dictionary which she finds utterly absorbing.)* Clear night.
MARIDOL. *(Absent-mindedly.)* Yes … *(Hanley looks back to see what is absorbing her.)*
HANLEY. What you got there?
MARIDOL. *(Holding it up.)* "Diksiyunario"! A teacher at the Ateneo *(Ah tay NAY o.)* wrote it. I never saw one before.
HANLEY. Lemme see that. *(He grabs the book and sits down beside*

31

her. Hanley begins to read aloud, pronouncing the words as an American would.)
HANLEY. "Bata. Boy. The boy is industrious." *(Stumbling.)* "Masipag ang batang lalaki." *(He looks at her.)* Think this is Greek?
MARIDOL. It *might* be Tagalog. *(Laughing.)* Let me see. *(Quickly.)* "Masipag ang batang lalaki." *(She pronounces it correctly — MAH-si-pahg ahng BAH-tang lah-LAH-kee.)*
HANLEY. Sounds like boilin' water to me. *(Pause.)* Bop — bop — bop. *(Maridol flips through the book.)*
MARIDOL. I think it will be very useful for you.
HANLEY. Useful to *me?* Whatever for?
MARIDOL. Look. "Batà" [BAH tah] — that is the word for child. "Batá" [Bah TAH] is to suffer. And bata [Ba-ta] is a robe. Listen. "Batà. Batá. Bata." *(They sound pretty similar. She smiles proudly.)* See? Now you will know the difference!
HANLEY. *(Incredulously. They all sound the same!)* Bata — bata — bata? *(She ignores him and traces the definitions on the pages happily.)*
MARIDOL. This book has *many* helpful words.
HANLEY. "Anggó — "
MARIDOL. *(Quickly correcting him grammatically.)* "Maangot."
HANLEY. *(Disregarding her.)* "The smell of spoilt milk." "Angí — the smell of burnt food." "Anghít — repulsive odor like that of a goat." *(Beat.)* "Coming mostly from the armpit." *(To her.)* They all sound the same too.
MARIDOL. But tell me — when you say these things in American, why do you need so many words?
HANLEY. *(He thinks.)* We don't have but one word for "smell." *(Pause.)* Well, there's "stench" ... and "stink." *(Beat.)* But none of them quite so specific ... *(He looks at the book again.)* Look here! "Bala" — that means bullet. *(He looks at her.)* They got the same word in Spanish.
MARIDOL. *(Simply.)* That is because we did not have bullets — until the Spanish came.
HANLEY. *(Letting it sink in.)* I see. *(She walks over to the map and looks at it thoughtfully.)*
MARIDOL. The Chinese. The Muslims. The Spanish. Now you. You each take something away, and you each leave something behind. *(Beat.)* "Zapatos"? Ah! So shoes were brought by the Spanish. *(Fiercely.)* But not "child," or "mountain," or "rain." Those are *our* words, and they will be here after all of you are gone.
HANLEY. You'n me should get some sleep. I've got my cot set up

32

out there. Even got me some sheets. *(He blows out one of the candles.)*
MARIDOL. *(Looking at Waller.)* I don't know … *(She goes to Waller and puts the back of her hand on his forehead. Worried, to Hanley:)* He is still very warm. *(She rinses the compress in the water and replaces it on Waller's brow. He opens his eyes and turns to stare at Hanley.)*
HANLEY. Major? *(Waller is silent and staring.)* Are you all right? *(Some of the following lines overlap. Waller looks at Hanley with disoriented urgency.)*
WALLER. You haven't shipped out?
HANLEY. Why, no sir … *(Waller's eyes search Hanley's face. At a loss. Anxiously to Maridol:)* Is he all right?
MARIDOL. I don't know. *(Waller shakes his head as though he's trying to rattle something out of it. Waller addresses Hanley with terrible intensity.)*
WALLER. You've got to look under the child.
HANLEY. What child?
WALLER. *(Blinking uncertainly at Hanley.)* Corporal?
HANLEY. *(With possible relief.)* Yes, sir.
WALLER. You understand?
HANLEY. No … I don't …
WALLER. *(Lost.)* That infantry captain shipping out last September, fresh outa West Point. Goin' on and on about his "philosophy" … "Be kind to the natives, treat 'em with respect — "
HANLEY. *(Worried, to Maridol.)* Should we give him more light?
MARIDOL. No! Look at his eyes! *(She speaks softly to Waller.)* Major …
WALLER. *(Struggling to put it together.)* It musta been late afternoon. Billy's posted at the gate. A procession comes along — native women with children's coffins. *(He shakes his head in confusion, then looks at Hanley differently.)* You make 'em open the lids. *(With pity.)* There's a dead little cholera child in every one. *(He looks at Hanley.)* You wave 'em through. They stack 'em right there in the church.
HANLEY. Major! I wasn't there.
WALLER. With bolo knives under — every one. *(With great sorrow, to Hanley.)* Why didn't you look *under* the child? *(Beat.)*
MARIDOL. Major, you should — *(Hanley motions for her to shush, Maridol gives him a look of dismay and Hanley looks intently at Waller to continue.)*
WALLER. Next morning my men are all sleeping … *(He stops short.)* No. You — were eating breakfast in the tent. The women — No! Insurgents dressed as women *(He stares wildly at Maridol.)* —

33

knock down our tents and start in to hack. *(Softly.)* Your captain's in his quarters, readin' his Bible. *(Beat.)* They hack off his head … and … finger. For the West Point … ring.

MARIDOL. *(Distressed.)* Major! Please don't!

HANLEY. *(To her.)* No! Let him speak!

WALLER. *(Slowly.)* Fifty-nine of our boys — die that day. *(Beat. Quietly:)* A few fight their way to the boats. *(He looks at Hanley and Maridol, full of pain and stunned wonder.)*

WALLER. And "the Greeks catch sight of the sea." *(Pause.)*

HANLEY. Your men? From China?

WALLER. No, son. *(Grieving.)* My boys are not among … the survivors. *(Pause.)*

HANLEY. Oh.

WALLER. Our relief party finds them in the tents … where they fell. *(A terrible image in his mind's eye.)* The only way they know *(He stares at Hanley, then closes his eyes and shakes himself.)* — Billy … is by my deck of cards … Our officer wires back: "Buried dead." *(Beat.)* "Burned town. *(Beat.)* "Returned."

HANLEY. And that when you gave 'em hell, right, Major?

MARIDOL. Corporal! He needs to stop!

HANLEY. *(Roughly pushing her aside.)* No! I want to hear!

WALLER. *(To Hanley.)* Chaffee sent me in, with his old Army buddy in command. *(Deliberately.)* General Jacob Smith. *(Pause.)*

HANLEY. *(Softly.)* Hell-Roarin … *(Waller nods.)*

WALLER. *(He now sees it.)* We are standing in a muddy field in Samar — me and — Hell-Roaring Jake. The island is drenched in stinking rain. This — *bog!* — is where they've thrown my men. *(Beat.)* The natives … have turned their hogs loose … on our burial ground. And they have torn it all asunder. *(In pain.)* I can see …

HANLEY. *(Sickened.)* — them?

WALLER. *(He shakes his head mildly. He looks toward Hanley's head.)* They were all … It's curious … how a scrap of red hair can … *(Silence. Hanley cringes, then suddenly pulls back. He dashes to the window, gulping lungfulls of air. Maridol puts out a hand to shake Waller gently, speaking softly but urgently.)*

MARIDOL. Major! Please wake up! *(Waller throws off her hand.)*

WALLER. I *am* awake, dammit! This is what I *see!* *(He returns to his mind's eye.)* And General Smith turns on me. He is a small man in stature, but he bellows like a bull. "I want no prisoners! I wish you to kill and burn!" *Those* were my *orders*. *(Quietly puzzled.)* And I'm thinkin' — "What am I to do?"

MARIDOL. *(Sorrowfully.)* Major. *(A long pause. Then Waller turns and looks at Hanley with a curious expression — almost a smile. His voice is gentle.)*

WALLER. You seem so very familiar ... *(Beat. He reaches a hand towards Hanley's hair.)* Is there not ... a reddish cast ... to your hair? *(Hanley bolts from the room — gagging? Waller stares ahead in catatonic stillness. Maridol nudges him towards the bed, and he moves towards it like a child or a sleepwalker.)*

MARIDOL. You can rest now. The breeze will come. *(Crooning. Maridol goes to her shelf and strokes the Virgin's feet. Then she picks up Quan Yin and inverts the figurine. She holds a finger beneath the drops that fall from her vessel. She goes to Waller and strokes the water lightly across his brow. He sits in the bed. Maridol waits for a moment, then kneels and quietly removes his boots. His feet are covered in bloody bandages. Maridol has a sharp intake of breath. Then she brings a basin of water over with a clean cloth. She unwraps them and bathes his feet gently.)*

WALLER. *(Absently.)* You needn't do this.

MARIDOL. It will help you sleep. *(She looks up at him.)* The breeze will come.

WALLER. It never comes ... *(Maridol dries his feet, then takes the basin and cloth back to the shelf. Waller bends his head into his hands and rocks in agitation. Maridol stands over him and lays her hands on his temples. His body slows its rocking and starts to relax. She begins to rub his head with her fingertips. He rocks yet more slowly. Maridol climbs on top of the bed. She arranges the mosquito net so it surrounds the bed. Maridol sits with legs crossed. She applies the compress to his head and leaves her hand on it. He starts up and stares at her in panic, but she quiets him. Waller gradually reclines, face to the ceiling, eyes closed, over her lap as she cradles him. The room fades to a dark blue, while the mosquito net glows from within with a silver light, making a pietá of Maridol and Waller, pale and luminous.)* ... Only accursèd rain.

MARIDOL. *(As to a child.)* Tonio. Tonio. *(Long pause.)*

WALLER. *(He starts up.)* I can't hear it. *(With great sadness Maridol rocks slowly, and begins to sing, as in a lullabye.)*

MARIDOL.

Ang bayan kung minamahal
Ang bayan kung *(Pause.)* Pilipinas
Sa dugo di nauunahan
Makamtan lang ang kalayaan

O bayan kung minumutya
Ako'y handang magpakasakit
Ang buhay ko'y nakalaan
Sa iyo mahal kung bayan
(See Appendix for song. Lights out.)

Scene 3

The Cold Light of Day

Lights up gradually to a pale yellow and pink early morning light. The shutters are only slightly open, and a clear bright light comes through them. Waller and Hanley sit at the table, focused on the chessboard. Waller is now fully dressed in his uniform, looking fresh and smart. At first glance he appears confident and purposeful. But he does still show signs of his ailments — his eyes still bother him and his head has occasional shooting pains. Maridol is lying on her side facing the audience, asleep on her straw mat, which has been spread out in front of Waller's bed. Her hair is loose but she wears the same dress. The basin and cloth are at her side. At her head stands the Madonna, with the two candles flanking her. The men speak in normal voices, though relatively quietly. Hanley advances a black piece towards Waller's side of the board.

HANLEY. I'm on my way. *(Hanley removes a white piece and looks up at Waller, almost gloating.)*
WALLER. *(With concern.)* Oh my. *(Waller advances a piece. Hanley advances his again, ever closer to Waller's king. He takes another black piece.)*
HANLEY. My king, your castle!
WALLER. Now look at that. *(Waller makes another move with white. Hanley looks at him, disbelieving.)*
HANLEY. *(Solicitously.)* Are you sure you want to do that?
WALLER. Why?
HANLEY. *(Shrugging.)* Oh, you know. You feelin' all right?

36

WALLER. No mercy, boy. You play for keeps.

HANLEY. All right … then … *(He moves a black piece.)* Check. Guess you didn't see it coming. *(Waller moves white. With the following exchanges each man moves his piece Waller's white pieces suddenly surround Hanley's black king.)*

WALLER. Now that was a good idea! *(Hanley glows. Waller moves.)* Check.

HANLEY. Oh! Wait. *(Moves.)*

WALLER. *(Moves.)* Check.

HANLEY. Damn! *(Moves.)* There.

WALLER. *(Moves.)* Checkmate. *(Waller stretches, ready to move on. Hanley is frozen, still absorbing his loss.)*

HANLEY. But you said that was a good idea.

WALLER. It was a good idea that didn't work — and in the Marines we call that a bad idea.

HANLEY. *(Scanning the board.)* But —

WALLER. *(Standing and stretching.)* Not bad, son, not bad at all. You've got potential. Now all you need is some skill.

HANLEY. *(Muttering, and trying for an instant replay, moving his hand over the pieces.)* My … rook, and his, uh, bishop. My pawn, his queen … and this here's a — ? *(Maridol wakes, sits up; shakes her head and blinks sleepily.)*

MARIDOL. *(To Waller.)* Oh! You are awake.

WALLER. Now you are too.

HANLEY. Well it's about time!

WALLER. *(As a stern reprimand.)* You leave her be. She was up half the night. *(Maridol kneels beside her mat and quickly rolls it up, removing all evidence of her presence. Waller idly walks over and picks up the statue of Quan Yin. He brings it back to the table and sits down to examine it in a technical fashion.)*

HANLEY. Will the Major be wantin' some breakfast? *(Maridol pins up her hair, swiftly and expertly. Then she takes her mat to its spot in the corner. She returns and picks up the Madonna and the candles, which she returns to the shelf. She looks at the shelf for a moment, puzzled. Then she looks at Waller and sees Quan Yin on the table in front of him. She is not pleased.)*

WALLER. You mean — like an *egg?* *(He grins.)* I think I'll pass. But I could do with some strong coffee. *(He reconsiders and grimaces south, with the state of his stomach in mind.)* No — make that … weak tea.

MARIDOL. I will bring it. *(Maridol exits. Waller looks after her.)*

WALLER. *(To Hanley.)* What's her name again?

HANLEY. Mary Dole, sir. Strange name for native, don't you think?

WALLER. Corporal, you're so fresh off the boat your feet're still wet. These Filipinos all have double-barreled names. They just chop 'em off and stick the pieces back together. Betcha a dime to a dollar she's "Maria de Somethin 'r other." *(Maridol comes in with a tray holding two cups and saucers. Her expression is opaque. She sets a cup in front of each man. Hanley's cup is already filled.)*

HANLEY. What's this?

MARIDOL. *(Impassively.)* Ginger root tea. I promised.

HANLEY. You can't expect me to drink this! Not after your last trick.

WALLER. *(Breaking in with command.)* — *I* would, soldier. Young woman knows what she's doing. *(Waller looks at her with a calculating gaze. Hanley takes a big sip of the ginger tea and makes a face. Waller smiles.)* I feel like a new man myself. *(Beat.)* But if it was the quinine, it certainly takes its toll …

MARIDOL. The quinine is necessary. But not sufficient. *(Waller looks at her with curiosity.)*

WALLER. You are uncommonly well spoken …

HANLEY. *(Sullenly.)* … for a native.

MARIDOL. My father studied in Europe. *(Beat.)* We had a plantation.

WALLER. *(Pleased, with great interest.)* A plantation. You don't say. Tobacco?

MARIDOL. *(Defiantly, in Hanley's direction.)* Coffee.

HANLEY. Well, coffee! What kind a crop is that?

WALLER. Quite a lucrative one —

MARIDOL. He was respected. *(Pause.)* They said that was what made him dangerous.

WALLER. *(He regards her seriously.)* I see. *(Beat.)* And you have studied the medical arts?

MARIDOL. Once I lost my family … I learned by watching. The Chinese doctor, the army surgeon. *(Beat.)* And the patients. Especially the patients.

WALLER. Yes. *(To Hanley.)* I have observed many an affliction. You have to *localize* the problem. And then excise it — with force and precision. Don't damage the neighboring tissue. Blunt instruments only *(Overlapping.)* spread the—

MARIDOL. *(Overlapping, looking intently at Waller.)* — the disease.

HANLEY. *(Clueless.)* Well, that's for sure. *(Beat. Cheerfully.)* And then you gotta amputate!

MARIDOL. *(Tonelessly.)* That is correct. *(Maridol and Waller exchange acute looks. She exits. Waller stands, wanders to the shelf and picks up Quan Yin.)*

WALLER. *(He looks back at Quan Yin. To Hanley:)* Ever see one a these?

HANLEY. No sir. Not before yesterday.

WALLER. They had 'em all over China. Look here. *(He picks up the glass.)* You pour water in the mouth of the fish down here, turn it upside down, and then it drips from the vase in her hand back into the fish. Drop by drop. "Like merciful rain from heaven." *(Beat.)* Wish I'd got one for my wife. *(Hanley sits down at the table, watching in fascination. He grabs for the statue.)*

HANLEY. Here, lemme see that! *(Waller pulls it back sharply.)*

WALLER. Soldier! *(Hanley has overstepped his bounds — and now he realizes it. He stands formally.)*

HANLEY. Sir!

WALLER. *(A stare, then he relents.)* Oh, just sit down. *(Beat.)* Here. *(Waller slides Quan Yin over to Hanley, who soon happily explores her like a young boy with a water toy. He looks up suddenly, disturbed.)*

HANLEY. That girl Mary Dole. *(Loud whisper.)* She told me she's Catholic. Do you think she worships this idol too?

WALLER. *(Shrugging.)* Can't say. I don't know if it's the statues they worship, or the water ...

HANLEY. *(Focused on the water.)* Drip ... *(Long pause.)* ... drip ... *(Beat.)* It's downright hypnotic. *(Maridol reenters with a Chinese teapot and sets it on the table. She sees Quan Yin on the table — her glance is sharp and possessive. She pours tea, then retreats to her corner.)*

WALLER. It is. *(Pause. He closes his eyes painfully.)* But it puts me in mind of the water cure.

HANLEY. *(Puzzled moment.)* I'm not sure I take your meaning. *(Waller is silent. Long pause.)* What does it cure?

WALLER. Oh ... the deaf, the dumb, and the mule-headed. *(Pause.)* They've been using it here for centuries. I believe it was invented ... by the Filipinos.

MARIDOL. No! By the Spaniards!

WALLER. *(To her, with mild curiosity.)* Is that so? *(Beat.)* Could be. *(Maridol is overcome by a memory and fights back tears, unnoticed.)*

HANLEY. *(With morbid fascination.)* How does it work? *(Waller inverts Quan Yin so the water drips, then turns her on her back to demonstrate the water cure. Maridol steps forward, wanting to rescue her, but stops herself. She watches, aghast.)*

WALLER. *(In a flat, technical voice.)* By forcing several gallons of water — sometimes salted — into the mouth and nose of the victim. Drop by drop. As a result of which the stomach ... will inflate.

HANLEY. Does he — die?

WALLER. Usually — not. Unless someone jumps on him. *(Beat.)* Usually he talks.

HANLEY. And that's what they did to your men? *(Waller sets Quan Yin upright abruptly. Maridol quietly retrieves her, carries her, cradled, to safety on the shelf.)*

WALLER. No soldier. They did not do that to my men ...

HANLEY. But I heard the reason you —

WALLER. The reason I *what?*

HANLEY. *(Catching himself.)* Nothing, sir!

WALLER. *(Temper rising.)* What did you hear, boy?

HANLEY. Lots of things! They just don't — add up.

WALLER. And who told you these "things"?

HANLEY. I don't know — it's just around town—and General Chaffee said you —

WALLER. So *Chaffee's* to be the arbiter of my reputation?

HANLEY. No, sir! They say you're —

WALLER. *(Rising and shouting.)* They say I'm what, boy?

HANLEY. *(Quietly.)* The "Butcher of Samar" sir. *(Beat.)* For havin' those prisoners shot.

WALLER. *(To Hanley.)* And you believe them?

HANLEY. *(Beat.)* I ... don't know what to believe. *(Waller sits down, defeated.)*

WALLER. *(With great weariness.)* "They say they say ... " *(Beat. To him:)* They *say* ... I'm the "hot topic" at all the Washington dinner parties. "Fix Waller and you've fixed the Philippines!" *(With consternation.)* They think their hands are clean?

HANLEY. I ... don't know.

WALLER. You *need* to know — what you're getting into.

HANLEY. I'll figure it out.

WALLER. Is that what Chaffee tells you? *(Waller looks at him for a long moment.)* They keep shipping you out, clean-scrubbed and ... *(Beat.)* down you go one by one. *(Long beat. He closes his eyes.)* I get to the point where — I don't even want to learn your names anymore. *(He looks away. Pause.)* My boys were cocky like you. When Chaffee sent us to Samar, I lined 'em up for a talking-to. *(Instructing his men.)* "Remember that West Point captain! Don't make his mis — " *(Pause. Waller closes his eyes in pain.)*

HANLEY. … mistake …

WALLER. *(Waller breathes, then continues.)* I had studied the character of the adversary. "They are treacherous, brave. And savage."

HANLEY. Brave? How can you say that?

WALLER. *(Nailing him with his gaze.)* Make no mistake. They are brave. *(Hanley looks briefly towards Maridol. She looks back steadily, then sits down in her chair in the corner — still listening.)* They sent us up the river to find the natives who attacked our base. Sixty Marines, with thirty natives to carry our provisions. Can't you see our problem? From the very start?

HANLEY. No … sir … I …

WALLER. Think, boy, think! What were those provisions?

HANLEY. Food?

WALLER. Yes. And bolos. To "cut through the brush"! The natives carried the bolos.

HANLEY. Sorry …

WALLER. Sorry won't help you. *(Beat.)* They were native *volunteers*. Why were they being so kind to us? So very very kind. Did we ask ourselves *why* they volunteered?

HANLEY. No?

WALLER. We did not. No white man had ever traveled that terrain. The mountain paths were steep and the rains poured down without mercy. Within days we were lost. Leeches. Cholera. Then we ran out of food. *(He sits.)* "So sorry," the natives said. *(He holds up empty hands.)* "Food gone." With that smile. Half the natives ran off, taking our weapons with them. My sick men started to die. *(Beat.)* One of them lost his reason. Just bolted …

MARIDOL. *(Quietly looking at her hands.)* It was the fever.

WALLER. I got the fever myself. We made camp, tried to save those we could. I'd wake up drenched in sweat, with another man dead at my side. And the natives standing over us. Silent. And watching.

HANLEY. They killed him?

WALLER. How were we to know? What was poison and what was the fever? *(Beat.)* But I couldn't take the risk.

HANLEY. So you had them shot.

WALLER. No, man! I put them under guard and sent them back to base. *(Deliberately.)* According to procedure. *(He gets up and starts to pace like a prosecutor.)* That's when the pieces came together. An Army officer at the base was investigating. He found out that — *(Pause.)* The insurgents we were hunting — were the natives at our

41

side! *(Beat.)* Imagine that. *(He shakes his head in disbelief.)* They had themselves a plan — a little crude perhaps, but it had worked before. Once they got rid of us, they could join the others in town. Then it was dead children in coffins with bolos underneath. To hack everyone on our base to pieces. *(Beat.)*

HANLEY. *(Confused.)* But they didn't.

WALLER. No. The town ringleaders confessed — the mayor, for God's sake! The constable. *(Beat.)* The priest! *(Maridol reacts.)* So our Army friend held 'im a little trial. And had them shot. *(Maridol crosses herself.)*

HANLEY. How'd he get them to confess?

WALLER. The water cure, man, the water cure!

MARIDOL. *(Bitterly.)* That's what they *all* use.

WALLER. I was laid up blind with fever, out in the bush. But the base was about to explode. Our prisoners were on the way back. If the townspeople overcame our guards, we would all be dead men. The officer sent me a message. "Recommend we shoot your prisoners too." *(Beat.)* Corporal.

HANLEY. Yes.

WALLER. What would *you* do?

HANLEY. I — I — don't —

WALLER. Can't you figure it out?

HANLEY. Well — I —

WALLER. Someone was goin' to die, and it wasn't gonna be my men. *(Quietly.)* So I ordered the prisoners shot in the town square. *(Coldly.)* And let the bodies lie where they fell. *(Pause.)* Which is more than they did for my men. *(Hanley looks away.)* So now I'm a butcher? *(Beat. Louder:)* That makes me a butcher? *(Beat. Louder:)* Answer me!

HANLEY. No. You can't ... I don't know! It's all — confused!

WALLER. *(Looking away, with bitter satisfaction.)* You want it all neat and tidy, just like the rest. But how can anyone look out for you if *nobody ever learns anything!*

MARIDOL. — What did they do?

WALLER. Pardon?

MARIDOL. The Pilipinos. What were they guilty of? *Looking* at you?

WALLER. No, girl! They were plotting to murder us. They confessed!

MARIDOL. After the water cure.

HANLEY. Conspiracy!

42

MARIDOL. No evidence. No trial. Just shot. Like my father.

HANLEY. That was the Spaniards. That was different.

MARIDOL. The water cure and the firing squad? What is different? *(Bitterly.)* You say you "bring the law."

WALLER. I couldn't let it happen again.

MARIDOL. And then you burned the town! And shot all the people!

WALLER. No! No. Just. Those ... eleven men. *(Quietly.)* Same as I'd lost in the jungle.

HANLEY. *(Reverently.)* It was Providential.

WALLER. *(To Hanley.)* So you see, my crime was not properly murder. I just forgot to hold me *a little trial!* (*General Chaffee appears quietly in the doorway. Hanley alone spots him, stands up and salutes and Chaffee dismisses him. The others do not notice.*)

HANLEY. So you *were* following orders ...

WALLER. My orders. Now that *is* amusing. You will recall the words of Hell-Roarin' Jake, at our burial ground.

CHAFFEE. *(In a dead voice.)* He told you "to kill and to burn." *(Hanley spots him first and stands at attention, though he does not salute.)*

HANLEY. Attention, general on deck. *(Waller stands at weary attention.)*

CHAFFEE. *(Acknowledging them.)* As you were.

WALLER. *(Relaxing, with ironic cordiality.)* Why, General Chaffee! *(Beat. Then, inclining his head with angry courtesy.)* Won't you come in?

HANLEY. *(Uncomfortably, to Chaffee.)* Sir!

WALLER. *(Beat.)* Thing is, I didn't, did I, General? *(Indicating Hanley.)* Jake Smith told me to burn the place down. My own lieutenant said he was gonna kill every goo-goo in town. I had to restrain him!

HANLEY. *(Looking from man to man uncertainly.)* But *you* were the one they prosecuted. *(Waller plays to Chaffee and Hanley at the same time, with different intent.)*

WALLER. True. But they nailed me on the wrong charge. It shoulda been for *disobeying* orders. *(To Hanley.)* Jake Smith told me — to kill anyone "*capable* of bearing arms against the United States." *(Beat.)* This sounded ... excessive ... to me. So I said, "General, what is the limit of age to respect?" And he said —

CHAFFEE. "Ten years."

WALLER. Kill anyone over ten — years — old. *(Pause.)* That man's a disgrace to his uniform. So yes. I disobeyed his orders. *(He*

sits down. There is a pause. Hanley picks up the statue of Quan Yin and mutely balances it in his hands. Maridol watches resentfully.)
CHAFFEE. *(Softly.)* The insurgents like to recruit young boys. You've seen it yourself. They don't know right from wrong, but they can do a whole lotta harm. *(Beat.)* Jake wasn't entirely wrong.
WALLER. I don't kill women and children.
CHAFFEE. *(With a distant air.)* I remember when the story hit the papers. I called Jake into my office and sat him down — just like the old days out West ... "Smith," I say. "Have you been having any *promiscuous* killing in Samar for fun?" *(Beat.)* He wouldn't answer ... and I'm thinkin', "Good Lord, here we go again."
WALLER. So you go after me.
CHAFFEE. You got the publicity! That damn fool lieutenant — you approve the order — and *he* goes around bragging about it. "I've seen me some action!" *(He looks deliberately at Hanley. Hanley looks uncomfortable.)* Right soldier?
HANLEY. I never meant it like that ...
CHAFFEE. — So he makes all the papers and *(To Hanley.)* our Major Waller was his commanding officer. *(Beat. To Waller:)* But you didn't have to drag poor old Jake into it.
WALLER. *(In cold fury.)* The *prosecution* called Jake Smith up to the stand. Was I supposed to sit there and watch him lie? He denied giving me those orders. He swore — under oath.
CHAFFEE. *(Looking away.)* Well.
WALLER. Well. *(Coldly explaining to Hanley.)* There happened to be witnesses. *(Pause.)* He happened — to put it in writing.
CHAFFEE. Jake can get — carried away. He was like that ... out West. *(Beat. Appealing:)* Waller, there are people back home who're trying to tear us to pieces. Newspapers all over us — Congress up in arms. We had to do something. *(Beat.)* I knew they'd go easy on you.
WALLER. *(Angrily.)* You want a real massacre? Take your pick — *(He walks over to the shelf, picks the newspaper on top.)* The Boston Journal. *(Beat. Waller looks to Chaffee, then Hanley.)* You know this one?
HANLEY. No, sir.
WALLER. Here's a little letter from a preacher's son — out in Batangas. *(He looks back to the paper.)* Seems he wrote his daddy about killin' — *(He squints down at the paper.)* ... some thirteen hundred insurgents."
CHAFFEE. That was in battle.
WALLER. Yes. *(He looks at him pointedly, then reads from the paper.)* "They called in a priest to hear their confession, then hung

the priest in front of the prisoners." *(Beat.)* " ... who then dug their own graves. Before they were gunned down in groups of twenty." *(Pause. He looks up.)* In battle.

CHAFFEE. That soldier — he took it back.

WALLER. You saw to that. *(To Hanley.)* But our soldier told his *Pa* it was an "act of mercy." *(Reading again.)* "With so much of the province burned — there was nothing to feed them."

CHAFFEE. *(Beat. Then appealing:)* Waller, you — of all people! — know what kind of enemy we're up against. They try to provoke us!

WALLER. I'm aware of that.

CHAFFEE. They distort the truth. They ambush us? *(Sarcastically.)* They're "heroes." We attack them? Oh — then they're "martyrs." *(Pause.)*

WALLER. And if civilians get in the way?

CHAFFEE. *They* don't respect civilians. Innocent people are their target. They like to use children. An American soldier sees a kid, he lets his guard down.

HANLEY. *(To himself softly.)* Like the coffins ...

CHAFFEE. And if we win this — *(He stops.)* When we win this thing, the Filipinos will be the first to benefit. We can drag them out of the dark ages. They just don't understand that yet.

WALLER. When do you think they will?

CHAFFEE. Who the hell knows? But if the insurgents turn people against us, we'll make damn sure there are consequences.

WALLER. So your "strategy" is to stoop to their level.

CHAFFEE. That was not the plan. *(Sotto voce.)* But you know the rule: "No plan survives first contact with the enemy." Do you want us in the Philippines forever? With a hundred Samar massacres? *(Beat.)* My God, you saw what they did to our boys! No human decency.

WALLER. *(Abstractly.)* Maybe ... that's how they even the odds ... *(He shrugs.)* Is it really so much worse? *(To Hanley, idly.)* Another test, boy. Which would you choose? A quick bolo through the neck, or bleeding slowly to death by the side of the road?

HANLEY. *(He turns his head, eyes closed, while he sees each scenario. Then, sickened:)* I can't say.

CHAFFEE. You leave him out of it!

WALLER. He's in it, General! *(Softly, to Hanley.)* Aren't you, boy. *(Hanley hangs his head.)* They can't match our weapons — so they invade our dreams. We can mortar a village 'til there's not a cat left to cry. But we can't seem to silence a severed head.

CHAFFEE. They're savages! And you gotta fight fire with fire!

WALLER. *(Shrugging.)* You think that'll work? I watched your Army in Virginia, General Chaffee. I was but a nine-year-old boy — not ten, mind you, just nine. But I can still smell the smoke ...

CHAFFEE. That's ancient history.

WALLER. Not for us. For every house you burn, there's a big ol' family wants you dead. For every prisoner you shoot, there's twenty kin — with long memories.

HANLEY. *(Looking from man to man anxiously.)* Twenty? *(Calculating quickly.)* For every — one?

WALLER. *(To Chafee.)* You don't want to be ... *excessive.*

CHAFFEE. There's one thing you left out. *(Beat.)* We have no alternative.

MARIDOL. You could go! *(Hanley moves to restrain her, but Chaffee dismisses the gesture with disdain. Continuing, in sorrow:)* You could all go back! ... to your towns, your territories, whatever they are ... You could just leave. *(Maridol sags to her knees. Chaffee approaches her with something resembling tenderness.)*

CHAFFEE. *(Gently.)* We couldn't do that, young lady. Abandon you to those crazy bolo-men? Leave you in hell's more like it! Wouldn't be right. *(Chaffee signals to Hanley to back off, and he gently offers a hand for her to stand. He speaks to her as if to a child.)* Oh, I know it's hard for you to imagine — what progress even looks like. *(Beat.)* Roads, schools, you have no idea. But you have to realize. Those young men who died, for your sake ... Samar. Batangas. For nothing? That's what we'd be saying, if we just up and walked away. *(Gently.)* We've got to set things straight. *(Beat. Then, to Waller.)* Don't we, Major.

WALLER. I can't see my way clear.

CHAFFEE. History will prove me right.

WALLER. You don't know that. *(He looks away, then back to Waller.)*

CHAFFEE. *(Beat.)* It's time to go.

WALLER. I am more than ready. *(He stands and prepares to go. Flinging his arms wide:)* Don't I get a blindfold?

CHAFFEE. *(Coldly.)* You exaggerate. Major. *(Beat.)* You didn't do so badly with that jury — near half of 'em are Marines. And the Army men — they're old Injun fighters. They know how it is.

WALLER. We'll see.

CHAFFEE. *(Fixed on Waller.)* — You know, Waller, you've busted open a real can a worms. Now they're going after Jake. *(Beat.)*

WALLER. Sounds right to me.

CHAFFEE. They'll go digging into Batangas ...

WALLER. You got something to hide?

CHAFFEE. You Marines are too close to the ground. Jump off the boat, run around and call a victory, then head for home. Don't see the big picture.

WALLER. We hit our mark. It's not our fault if other folk don't know where to aim.

CHAFFEE. *(Looks at Waller with quiet fury.)* You think it was my call? I know you're a Marine — but haven't you heard of chain of command? Some people in Washington think we can wage a clean little war against an enemy who plays dirty. And Major, you spoil the picture. *(Waller picks up his valise.)*

WALLER. You know, General, the Filipinos have a deadly weapon. It's a *disk* with sharpened edges — razor sharp — and a rope wrapped 'round. You hurl it at your enemy, then pull it back in. *(Beat.)* It's called a "yo-yo" ... You just gotta watch yourself once it starts back. *(Chaffee goes out the door, then turns to look back. Waller starts out. He takes a step and winces slightly as his foot begins to buckle, but instantly recomposes himself and goes on. Hanley hesitates, then salutes him. He has changed sides.)*

HANLEY. Good luck, Major. *(Waller steps back, shaking his head in embarrassment.)*

WALLER. Now where are my manners? Soldier, good luck to you. I'll stand you a drink sometime. *(Beat.)* In the future.

HANLEY. *(Still saluting.)* Yes sir.

WALLER. *(To Maridol.)* And I thank you for your attentions. Maria de —

MARIDOL. — los Dolores. *(Waller holds out his hand. Hanley grudgingly reaches into his pocket for the dime to pay his bet, and hands it over. Waller takes it and exits.)*

Scene 4

Rough Justice

Lights up on Chaffee, sitting on a wooden chair to the left of the stage, facing the audience impassively. He has a side table and a gavel, as well as a small, dog-eared manual. An identical chair stands at center stage, with a blinding spotlight fixed on it. Waller enters from stage right. He almost manages to disguise his limp and shows his accustomed military bearing. He faces the audience and tries to search the faces, but the spotlight oppresses his gaze. He is not as unflinching as he would like. There is the sound of slow-dripping water. Rain?

CHAFFEE. *(Striking the gavel.)* The Court Martial will come to order; all parties and members are present. *(Chaffee looks to the audience, sternly signaling to sit down and be silent. Waller is uncertain for a moment, then sits, facing forward. Reading from the manual:)* Major Waller, would you and your counsel stan — *(He looks up and realizes the need to correct himself, and looks back down to the manual.)* Major Waller, would you stand up please and approach the Board. *(Waller stands and walks over to Chaffee. He closes his eyes and waits.)* Major Waller, this court-martial *(He glances stonily over to the area where the jury would be sitting, then goes back to the manual.)* finds you of all specifications and charges: *(Long pause.)* Not Guilty.
WALLER. *(Opens his eyes in amazement.)* Not guilty? Well, then … *(He looks around, happy and proud. But he is met with no cheers, only silence. He is still alone. Looking around, insistently.)* Not guilty. *(He makes a conciliatory gesture towards Chaffee, but Chaffee stands, crosses his arms, still holding the manual, and turns his back on him. Now distraught.)* He said not guilty! I won my case! *(He looks around again, less certain.)* But I won … *(Again, silence. Waller closes his eyes again, disoriented. The spotlight keeps getting brighter, unbearably bright. He blinks and starts to leave but is paralyzed by confusion. He stumbles and sinks back into his chair.)*
CHAFFEE. *(Half to himself.)* That's the thing, Major. If you take on the law, you wanna know how to plead. *(He looks Waller up and*

48

down, into his feverish eyes.) Well, soon you'll be back in the world. *(Chaffee turns briskly and walks out. Waller stares out to the audience.)* WALLER. A Marine. Does not plead. *(Blackout on Waller. There is the first sound of thunder in the distance.)*

Scene 5

The Rainy Season

It is a few days later — late morning, in the same room. The sky is now cloudy, and thunder sounds in the distance at various points throughout the scene. Hanley is sitting at the table, going over a newspaper. He is wearing his side arm. Maridol is on her knees on the floor, carefully wrapping a bolo in white cloth before placing it in a wooden packing case.

HANLEY. *(Grinning.)* Acquitted — eleven to two. The major must feel fine.
MARIDOL. *(Impassively.)* I do not understand your trials.
HANLEY. *(Distantly.)* I wonder if you can convert. From Army to Marine.
MARIDOL. Where is he going with so many things?
HANLEY. *(Suddenly noticing her wrapping the bolo.)* Hey, watch yourself there — that's dangerous.
MARIDOL. I will be careful.
HANLEY. It's sposed to be down to the dock before noon. I guess he's shipping out. Bet he can't wait!
MARIDOL. Where is he going?
HANLEY. I dunno. *(Proudly.)* Whatever front's heatin' up. *(He returns to the newspaper. Maridol finishes packing. She moves around the room, closing the cases, one by one, as Hanley tries not to watch but is vaguely disturbed. She goes to the mantel and picks up the Madonna and Quan Yin, wraps them carefully and puts them in her bag. Hanley is working through the newspaper. He's doing better with his reading, though his lips still move slightly. Shocked:)* Hold on a minute … The Major's got a new assignment. *(Beat.)* He'll be — recruiting!
MARIDOL. Oh?

HANLEY. *(In consternation.)* In New Jersey.

MARIDOL. Oh. *(Mildly.)* Is that front heating up?

HANLEY. *(Crushed.)* But he was acquitted!

MARIDOL. *(Flat.)* I do not understand your trials. *(A long pause. She regards him. He is silent.)* What about you, Han Li? Where will you go now?

HANLEY. *(With trepidation.)* I was sposed to go to Batangas. *(A note of fear.)* But now they say — Zamboanga. *(He rubs his neck.)*

MARIDOL. Monkeys.

HANLEY. *(With a note of embarrassment.)* Monkeys. *(Hanley looks around and realizes the silence and emptiness of the room. He is full of finger-drumming nervous energy.)* Hey Mary Dole. I was thinkin' … maybe you could stick around for a while, just to … help out.

MARIDOL. Help what?

HANLEY. Oh, I don't know … I don't ship out 'til next month. *(Pause. He looks around nervously.)* I can't see rattlin' around here by myself.

MARIDOL. *(She pauses.)* I am free to go, am I not? You say you came to free us, so I must be free.

HANLEY. *(Long pause. Forlorn:)* They say it's like a gopher hole.

MARIDOL. It is you who are prisoners here.

HANLEY. You swat 'em down in Batangas and up they pop in Samar.

MARIDOL. Poor soldiers.

HANLEY. Swat 'em down in Samar. And there they are in Mindanao …

MARIDOL. *(Distantly.)* I do not know these … gophers. *(Maridol goes to the window and looks out.)*

HANLEY. Bang-bang Batangas. *(Thinks.)* Y'know, I don't really have a picture of Bantangas. Way they talk about it, sounds like — hell. All smoke and ruin. *(Embarrassed.)* Guess that's not how you see it. *(Maridol is deep in memory.)*

MARIDOL. What if I told you there were orchids on the road to my house? And that coffee blossoms are white, and smell like jasmine?

HANLEY. *(Closing his eyes.)* You got a real house?

MARIDOL. With a sitting room. *(She looks around with familiarity.)* My harp, in the corner. And white lace. We wear *(She touches her bodice.)* fine white lace. *(She closes her eyes tightly. Hanley breaks the spell.)*

HANLEY. Sure. And everyone's happy and dives for gray pearls.

MARIDOL. *(She opens her eyes and looks him square on.)* No, Han

50

Li. *(Long beat. With great deliberation:)* Our workers are hungry. And die very young.

HANLEY. No heaven.

MARIDOL. *(She shakes her head disparagingly. She looks at him with almost pity.)* Why do you go looking your heavens and your hells? It's just who we are. Just — Batangas. *(Maridol shakes herself back to the present, and looks toward the door. She picks up her bag and starts to leave. There is a sound of bottles and Hanley notices that it seems unusually heavy. Suddenly Hanley moves to physically restrain her.)*

HANLEY. *(Now suspicious.)* Hey! What's that? *(He holds her arm and pulls the bag from her.)*

MARIDOL. I go now. Let me go. *(Hanley puts the bag on the floor, kneels down and tears it open. Quan Yin is on top. He grasps the figurine in his hand to look beneath it. He pulls out items as he names them.)*

HANLEY. Quinine. Bandages. Laudanum! *(He stares up at her accusingly.)* This here's Army property!

MARIDOL. I call it payment.

HANLEY. *(Looking at her with new eyes.)* And where do you think you're taking it? To your *plantation? (She is briefly silent. He stands, grasping Quan Yin harshly in his hand. The following lines build, overlapping. The italicized words emerge with special clarity.)*

MARIDOL. No, Han Li. *(Dully.)* The *boys* from Kansas. *(Beat.)* They *burned* it —

HANLEY. — No —

MARIDOL. *(Raising her voice in despair.)* — They burned *every-thing.*

HANLEY. — Stop —

MARIDOL. *(In anguish.)* They took my *brothers* to the *bridge* and *shot* them —

HANLEY. *(Shouting.)* I don't want to hear this.

MARIDOL. — And threw their *bodies* in the *river. (Beat.)*

HANLEY. *(Thinking. Fast. With uncertainty:) Insurgents.* They musta been … insurgents …

MARIDOL. *(Standing her ground.)* I'm taking it to the *camps* —

HANLEY. — to give *aid* and comfort to the *enemy* —

MARIDOL. — they have *malaria! (Silence. Then, with force.)* My *people* are dying!

HANLEY. Our *boys* are dying too! *(Beat.)* Don't you have any *loyalty? (Maridol moves towards him and grabs the Quan Yin statue, trying to pull it away from him.)*

MARIDOL. *(She spits it out.)* To you? *(Beat.)* I have *utang na loob!* [OO-tahng nah loe-OBE] *(Hanley makes a threatening gesture with Quan Yin. Wailing and moving towards him:)* Give her back!

HANLEY. You can go to hell. *(Hanley pulls the statue violently back and dashes it to the floor where it shatters into pieces. Maridol runs to the pieces and kneels over them, crying out in a long, anguished keen.)*

MARIDOL. No-o-o-o! *(Maridol picks up the pieces, heart-broken. Distraught:)* Why do you have to *break* everything? *(She futilely tries to put the pieces back together and lets out a sharp cry — "Ayyy!" Her hand has been cut. She quickly raises her hand to her mouth.)*

HANLEY. *(Concerned.)* Hey! Let me see that. *(He goes to her with great concern and takes her hand to look at it. She resists him, mourning and rocking back and forth.)*

MARIDOL. Go away!

HANLEY. I know what to do — gimme that hand, Mary Dole.

MARIDOL. *(With less certainty.)* Stay away from me ... *(Gradually she relents, allowing him to take her hand and examine it.)*

HANLEY. Now look here, I'll just ... *(Without relinquishing her hand, he reaches out and picks up rubbing alcohol from her bundle, then a cloth and white bandage and tape.)* ... get that sharp bit out ... *(She pulls away and he settles her.)* Now hold on! *(She sits quietly and watches him treat her hand with surprise — he is more competent than she expects.)*

MARIDOL. *(Tonelessly.)* You know how to clean a wound.

HANLEY. *(Beat. Looking at her hand.)* Done it before. *(He looks away in pain.)* In Cuba. *(He finishes. They lock in an intense look. She stands. She sharply gathers her things together and turns to confront him. He stands with large fragments of Quan Yin in one hand, his other on his pistol.)*

MARIDOL. *(With hostility.)* What are you going to do now, corporal? Shoot me?

HANLEY. *(Bereft. Conflicted. He takes a deep breath.)* Go! *(They stand off and lock eyes in a long, intense glance that encompasses many conflicting emotions. Then Hanley closes his eyes, clenches, and emits a long deafening bellow of pain and frustration.)* Go-o-o-o! *(Maridol leaves. Hanley looks at the fragments of Quan Yin in his hand. He doesn't know what to do with them. Lights out.)*

End of Play

PROPERTY LIST

Whisky carafe
Two small tumblers
Old map of Philippines (with surrounding region: Hong Kong,
Indonesia)
Camp bed against the wall
Small stand with a candle
Mosquito net
Waller's initialed portmanteau
2 books
Knick-knack shelf
Embroidery/sewing
Some old newspapers.
A wooden tray
A plain bowl (of soup)
A spoon
Two forks
Two plates (of noodles)
Two large eggs, one prepared with "bones" and feather.
Antique-looking Madonna figurine
A porcelain Quan Yin that drips water
Two small votive candles
Pocketwatch
Medical supplies — bottles and bandages
Bolo knives
Packing cases
Pistol and holster

PRONUNCIATIONS

Samar — SA mar

Tagalog — Ta GA log

Maridol Amaya (as said by her.) — Mah-ri DOL ah MY ah

Pasig — PAH sig

Insurrecto — In sur REC toe

Kipuya — Ki POO ya

Tagalog words with "ang" should be pronounced with a soft "g" by Maridol (as in "banging," but a hard "g" by the Americans — "Batang-gas")

HISTORICAL CHRONOLOGY

Late 1890s. Concern in the US builds over the Cuban insurrection against the Spanish colonial government. The Spanish military forces take harsh measures against both the guerrilla and the civilian population. The Filipino independence movement makes significant inroads against the Spanish colonial regime.

February 15, 1898. The *USS Maine* explodes and sinks in Havana Bay, killing 264 American sailors and two officers. The Spanish government pleads innocence and offers compensation, but in the US, momentum builds to go to war. (A 1976 Navy investigation led by Admiral Hyman Rickover concluded that the probable cause was a faulty boiler on board.)

April 21, 1898. Hostilities between the US and Spain begin over Cuba. Filipino independence forces step up their activities against the Spanish.

May 1, 1898. Filipino forces make major inroads against the Spanish. Seeking to limit Spain's naval capacity in the Caribbean, Admiral Dewey and the US Navy win a dramatic victory over the Spanish fleet in Manila Bay in the Philippines.

June 12, 1898. Filipino leader Emilio Aguinaldo declares the birth of the independent republic of the Philippines in Manila.

June 24, 1898. In Cuba, US forces land on the southern coast and attack the town of Las Guásimas.

July 1, 1898. The Rough Riders, a volunteer cavalry organized by assistant Secretary of the Navy Theodore Roosevelt and Army Colonel Leonard Wood, participate in an attack on San Juan Hill. (Regular army troops take San Juan Hill — the Rough Riders take the less euphonious Kettle Hill.)

July 3, 1898. US Navy vessels, including the USS *Indiana*, where Littleton Waller is stationed, attacks the Spanish fleet in Santiago Bay, a few miles from the Rough Riders' position.

August 12, 1898. An Armistice ends the four-month war with Spain.

Spain cedes all claim on its territories in the Western Hemisphere. The US takes control of Cuba and Puerto Rico as its own colonial possessions. Discussions continue regarding the Philippines. President McKinley considers making the Philippines independent but maintaining a claim to a port in Manila as a fueling station.

October 24, 1898. President William McKinley wakes up in the middle of the night and claiming he's heard the voice of God telling him to keep the entire Philippine Islands. "Take them all to educate [and] ... Christianize the Filipinos," he heard.

December 10, 1898. US Secretary of State John Hay signs peace treaty in Paris. The US purchases the Philippines for 20 million dollars, and Spain cedes Cuba, Guam and Puerto Rico. Nationalists in Cuba, Puerto Rico, and the Philippines all protest — the Filipinos with special vehemence.

February 4, 1899. Amid building tensions, Nebraska sentry Willie Grayson fires upon and kills several Filipinos who ignore his command. The response sparks an armed revolt against the American occupation.

March 1899. Army Provost Arthur McArthur (father of Douglas McArthur.) institutes massive civic action and public works programs in Manila, including public health measures, vaccinations, food distribution, schools, and weekly inspections of prostitutes. Courts are reopened.

June 1899. US volunteer forces begin to dwindle with low rates of reenlistment. New troops, including black regiments, are recruited to replace them. Due to the 1893 bank failures and the depression, many unemployed young men from the farm states go into the military — which has been expanded almost tenfold in five years.

General Henry Lawton persuades the War Department to "Filipinize" the conflict by recruiting "scouts" from the Macabebe people to support the American troops, against their traditional Tagalog enemies.

September 9, 1899. US Army officer J. Franklin Bell is awarded the medal of honor for actions in Porac, Luzon. He was wounded in action several months earlier.

December 15, 1899. Major Littleton Waller and a contingent of Marines arrive in Manila and are based in Cavite.

December 18, 1899. General Henry Lawton is killed by an *insurrecto* sharpshooter fighting under the command of General Lucerio Geronimo.

1900. American forces carry out combined operations of counterinsurgency and public works in the Philippine Islands.

Spring 1900. US military uniforms in the Philippines, made of wool, are replaced by khaki cotton.

July 1900. Littleton Waller leads a small American force, including members of the Ninth Army Infantry, in a joint operation in Tientsin, China, in response to the Boxer Rebellion, a movement attempting to expel European colonial powers from China. Serving under the command of General Adna Chaffee, Waller is highly praised for his leadership.

November 1900. President McKinley is reelected with Theodore Roosevelt as his running mate, thanks to the political benefits of the publicity won by the Rough Riders.

March 28, 1901. Littleton Waller is brevetted Lieutenant Colonel for his gallant service in the Battle of Tientsin. (A brevetted rank was the equivalent of today's medals, but did not translate in terms of actual rank and authority.) He is regarded as a rising star in the Marines.

May 2, 1901. The New York Times publishes an interview with General J. Franklin Bell, the West Point graduate who commanded the scorched earth campaign in Batangas, who states that one-sixth of the population of Luzon has been killed or died of dengue in the previous two years under US occupation. (Historians later revised the figure to one in eight.)

September 5, 1901. President McKinley is shot by anarchist Leon Czolgosz in Buffalo. He lingers for a few days and dies. Theodore Roosevelt, 42, becomes the youngest president in US history.

September 28, 1901. Army Captain Thomas Connell, recently returned from China, commands a unit from the Ninth Infantry in the port town of Balangiga on Samar, one of the Visayan islands of the Philippines. Connell, an admirer of McKinley, is deeply upset by his death, and is planning a memorial prayer service when his troops are ambushed by *insurrectos.* Connell and 58 of his men are killed and their bodies horribly mutilated. (Some 250 villagers are killed in the incident.)

October 1901. Army General "Howling Jake" (or "Hell Roaring Jake") Smith brings Marine Major Littleton Waller to Samar to command a series of search-and-destroy missions. Between October 23 and November 30, Smith gives Waller a series of verbal and written orders to turn the interior of Samar into a "howling wilderness."

Late 1901. General Smith tells press that he intends to have island of Samar burned.

October 1901 – February 26, 1902. Waller, under orders to pursue the insurgents and seek a route for an army telegraph line, leads his men through the wilderness of Samar with disastrous results, but manages to save some. Several of the American survivors are so traumatized by the experience that they spend years in a government hospital for the insane. Waller's Filipino guide for the mission, "Victor," turns out to be one of the insurgents involved in other attacks. The army investigation at the base reveals that many of the town's leading officials are involved in the conspiracy.

December 7, 1901. Bell begins his "concentration camp" strategy in Batangas. He institutes "dead lines" around townships — any Filipino who crosses one without giving himself up to US troops is killed, and everything outside them is destroyed through a scorched earth policy. (The term "deadline" is borrowed from the notorious Andersonville prison in the Civil War, and is later adopted by journalists.)

January 1902. Senator Hoar, reacting in part to news reports of General Jake Smith's threats to devastate Samar, begins a Congressional investigation of the conduct of the war by the standing committee on the Philippines headed by Henry Cabot Lodge.

January 20, 1902. Waller is laid up with fever. His lieutenant sends him a message recommending the execution of eleven prisoners in the village of Basey. Waller agrees. He ships out to Manila a month later.

February 26, 1902. Waller is relieved of duty. He is shipped back to Manila on the transport ship, *Lawton.* Navy vessels dipped their flags in salute.

March 2, 1902. Waller arrives back in Manila.

March 17 – April 12, 1902. Waller's court-martial takes place in Manila, as a result of political pressure on General Adna Chaffee, military governor of the islands. Waller is acquitted by a vote of 11–2, after he is driven to disclose General Smith's orders to "kill and burn." One of the grounds for his acquittal is a Civil War-era regulation that permits prisoners of war to be killed if they are judged to present an immediate threat to those holding them.

April 16, 1902. General Malvar surrenders to General J. Franklin Bell in Batangas. (They later become good friends.)

April 24 – May 3, 1902. Brigadier General Jacob Smith is court-martialed in Manila. He is convicted and leaves the army, but receives a hero's welcome on his trip back to the U.S.

May 1902. Major Edwin Glenn is court-martialed in Catbalogan, Samar for the use of the "water cure" in Igbarras, Panay, and for wantonly burning the town. He is suspended for one month and fined 50 dollars. (A mainland newspaper points out that this is half the fine imposed for spitting on a streetcar in Boston.)

May 2, 1902. *The New York Times* reflects on the Congressional hearings: "A choice of cruelties is the best that has been offered in the Philippines It is not so certain that we at home can afford to shudder at the "water cure" unless we disdain the whole job. The army has obeyed orders. It was sent to subdue Filipinos. Having the devil to fight, it has sometimes used fire."

May 4, 1902. Waller and 200 marines leave Manila for San Francisco on the US *Warren.*

May 5, 1902. The Boston *Journal* publishes a letter from an American soldier in the Philippines to his father, Rev. W.H. Walker, who ran a missionary school in Boston. The letter (approvingly.) describes the systematic execution of 1,300 prisoners in Batangas. A priest had been called in to hear their confessions, and was then hung in view of the prisoners. They then dug their own mass graves before being gunned down in groups of twenty. The soldier reports that the reason for killing the prisoners is that, with much of the province burned, there is nothing to feed them.

June 14, 1902. Warren and the Marines report to the Brooklyn Navy Yard.

July 4, 1902. President Theodore Roosevelt declares the end of the war in the Philippines.

July 31, 1902. The San Francisco *Call* quotes a former Army contract surgeon, Dr. Henry Rowland, who explained American atrocities as "the tropical and vertical sun impairing the judgment" of men from cooler climates. As a result of the heat, "it does not take the American soldier, from private to general, long to conceive of the "insurrectos" as vermin, only to be ridded by extermination."

Fall 1902. Major Edwin Glenn is tried again, this time for the murder of 47 prisoners. A witness describes how he had ordered his victims to kneel and "repent of their sins" before they were bayoneted and clubbed to death. Glenn does not deny the charges, but states he was following Chaffee's order to obtain information on the insurrection "no matter what measures have to be adopted." He is acquitted on this defense. (Glenn is later promoted to General. A highway is named after him in Alaska.)

Late 1902. The US government discontinues all further courts martial as part of the "exit strategy."

1903. Army Chief of Staff Nelson Miles publishes a report of his inspection tour of the Philippines, in which he criticizes General Bell's concentration camps, which crammed more than 600 people into a space of seventy feet by twenty feet, resulting in deaths by suffocation. Bell's measures are reckoned to have led to the deaths of over 100,000 people. Miles' charges are dismissed by the press and discouraged by President Roosevelt. Miles reaches retirement age and departs quietly.

Chaffee, on a visit back to the US, gives a speech stating "Thanks to Jake Smith, Samar was more peaceful than many parts of the United States." He jokes about the "severe measures" in store for the Moro "agricultural savages" of the "Mohamedian [sic] faith" in Mindinao, who have not yet surrendered to US forces. "They do not wish to come into contact with us, but we love them and are going to tell them so."

Adna Chaffee is promoted to chief of staff, the highest rank of the US Army. He becomes the first enlisted man to rise to the top rank in the service. He retires at his own request two years later, after more than 40 years in the service. He is replaced by General J. Franklin Bell, who instigated the Batangas concentration camps.

March 7, 1906. US troops under the command of General Leonard Wood attack a tribe of insurgent Moros, who were holed up in the crater of an extinct volcano at Mount Dajo on Jolo. Members of the tribe had conducted a series of fatal raids on US soldiers. The tribe, armed only with swords and knives, was given several chances to surrender, and to send the women and children to safety, but they refused. In the ensuing US assault, all of the Filipinos, estimated at between 900 and 1600 men, women and children, were killed. (One account states that six men survived.) American forces suffered 15 dead and 32 wounded. President Theodore Roosevelt sent a telegram praising Wood for "the brave feat of arms wherein you and the officers and men under your command upheld the honor of the American flag."

June 1913. An end to hostilities on Mindanao is announced, but fighting continues sporadically for decades.

1940. US Army establishes Fort Chaffee in Arkansas, named in honor of Adna Chaffee. Fort Leonard Wood is established in Missouri the same year. The USS *James Franklin Bell,* an attack transport, serves from 1940–1945. The USS *Waller,* a destroyer, serves from 1942-1946, and again from 1950–1969. The *Waller* is one of the escorts for the Bay of Pigs invasion. It is finally decommissioned and sunk as a target off the coast of Rhode Island in 1970.

MONKEYS HAVE NO TAILS IN ZAMBOANGA

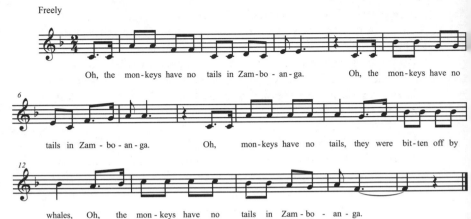

Freely

Oh, the mon-keys have no tails in Zam-bo - an - ga. Oh, the mon-keys have no

tails in Zam - bo - an - ga. Oh, mon-keys have no tails, they were bit-ten off by

whales, Oh, the mon-keys have no tails in Zam-bo - an - ga.

MONKEYS HAVE NO TAILS IN ZAMBOANGA

Oh, the monkeys have no tails in Zamboanga,
Oh, the monkeys have no tails in Zamboanga,
Oh, the monkeys have no tails,
They were bitten off by whales,
Oh, the monkeys have no tails in Zamboanga.

Oh, the carabao have no hair in Mindanao,
Oh, the carabao have no hair in Mindanao,
Oh, the carabao have no hair,
Holy smoke! But they are bare,
Oh, the carabao have no hair in Mindanao.

MARIDOL'S SONG

Softly, with emotion

Ang ba-yan kung mi - na - ma-hal, Ang ba-yan kung Pi - lii - pi - nas   Sa du-go di na-un-

a-han Ma - kam-tan lang ang ka-la - ya-an   O   ba-yan kung mi - nu-mut - ya Ak - o'y han-dang mag-pa-ka-

sa - kit   Ang bu-hay ko'y   na - ka-la-an   Sa   i - yo ma-hal kung   ba - yan

64

TRANSLATION OF MARIDOL'S SONG
(Traditional)

My precious country, my country, Philippines,
Blood has been spilled trying to grasp freedom.

My beautiful country, my country Philipines,
I am ready to bear suffering for your sake
I am ready to lay down my life for you,
beloved country.

Ang bayan kung minamahal
[bayan=country, (mina.) mahal=precious]
Ang bayan kung Pilipinas
Sa dugo di nauunahan
[dugo=blood, pinuhunanan=spilled out]
Makamtan lang ang kalayaan
[(ma.) kamtan=to grasp, kalayaan=freedom]

O bayan kung minumutya
[minumutya=very beautiful]
Ako'y handang magpakasakit
[handang=ready, (magpa=to me.) sakit=pain/suffering]
Ang buhay ko'y nakalaan
[buhay=life, nakalaan=to offer]
Sa iyo mahal kung bayan.

American Marine officer in the Philippines, circa 1900.

Filipinos, circa 1900.

NEW PLAYS

★ **THE GREAT AMERICAN TRAILER PARK MUSICAL music and lyrics by David Nehls, book by Betsy Kelso.** Pippi, a stripper on the run, has just moved into Armadillo Acres, wreaking havoc among the tenants of Florida's most exclusive trailer park. "Adultery, strippers, murderous ex-boyfriends, Costco and the Ice Capades. Undeniable fun." *–NY Post.* "Joyful and un-ashamedly vulgar." *–The New Yorker.* "Sparkles with treasure." *–New York Sun.* [2M, 5W] ISBN: 978-0-8222-2137-1

★ **MATCH by Stephen Belber.** When a young Seattle couple meet a promi-nent New York choreographer, they are led on a fraught journey that will change their lives forever. "Uproariously funny, deeply moving, enthralling theatre." *–NY Daily News.* "Prolific laughs and ear-to-ear smiles." *–NY Magazine.* [2M, 1W] ISBN: 978-0-8222-2020-6

★ **MR. MARMALADE by Noah Haidle.** Four-year-old Lucy's imaginary friend, Mr. Marmalade, doesn't have much time for her—not to mention he has a cocaine addiction and a penchant for pornography. "Alternately hilarious and heartbreaking." *–The New Yorker.* "A mature and accomplished play." *–LA Times.* "Scathingly observant comedy." *–Miami Herald.* [4M, 2W] ISBN: 978-0-8222-2142-5

★ **MOONLIGHT AND MAGNOLIAS by Ron Hutchinson.** Three men cloister themselves as they work tirelessly to reshape a screenplay that's just not working—*Gone with the Wind.* "Consumers of vintage Hollywood insider stories will eat up Hutchinson's diverting conjecture." *–Variety.* "A lot of fun." *–NY Post.* "A Hollywood dream-factory farce." *–Chicago Sun-Times.* [3M, 1W] ISBN: 978-0-8222-2084-8

★ **THE LEARNED LADIES OF PARK AVENUE by David Grimm, trans-lated and freely adapted from Molière's *Les Femmes Savantes.*** Dicky wants to marry Betty, but her mother's plan is for Betty to wed a most pompous man. "A brave, brainy and barmy revision." *–Hartford Courant.* "A rare but welcome bird in contemporary theatre." *–New Haven Register.* "Roll over Cole Porter." *–Boston Globe.* [5M, 5W] ISBN: 978-0-8222-2135-7

★ **REGRETS ONLY by Paul Rudnick.** A sparkling comedy of Manhattan manners that explores the latest topics in marriage, friendships and squandered riches. "One of the funniest quip-meisters on the planet." *–NY Times.* "Precious moments of hilarity. Devastatingly accurate political and social satire." *–BackStage.* "Great fun." *–CurtainUp.* [3M, 3W] ISBN: 978-0-8222-2223-1

DRAMATISTS PLAY SERVICE, INC.
440 Park Avenue South, New York, NY 10016 212-683-8960 Fax 212-213-1539
postmaster@dramatists.com   www.dramatists.com

NEW PLAYS

★ **AFTER ASHLEY by Gina Gionfriddo.** A teenager is unwillingly thrust into the national spotlight when a family tragedy becomes talk-show fodder. "A work that virtually any audience would find accessible." –*NY Times.* "Deft characterization and caustic humor." –*NY Sun.* "A smart satirical drama." –*Variety.* [4M, 2W] ISBN: 978-0-8222-2099-2

★ **THE RUBY SUNRISE by Rinne Groff.** Twenty-five years after Ruby struggles to realize her dream of inventing the first television, her daughter faces similar battles of faith as she works to get Ruby's story told on network TV. "Measured and intelligent, optimistic yet clear-eyed." –*NY Magazine.* "Maintains an exciting sense of ingenuity." –*Village Voice.* "Sinuous theatrical flair." –*Broadway.com.* [3M, 4W] ISBN: 978-0-8222-2140-1

★ **MY NAME IS RACHEL CORRIE taken from the writings of Rachel Corrie, edited by Alan Rickman and Katharine Viner.** This solo piece tells the story of Rachel Corrie who was killed in Gaza by an Israeli bulldozer set to demolish a Palestinian home. "Heartbreaking urgency. An invigoratingly detailed portrait of a passionate idealist." –*NY Times.* "Deeply authentically human." –*USA Today.* "A stunning dramatization." –*CurtainUp.* [1W] ISBN: 978-0-8222-2222-4

★ **ALMOST, MAINE by John Cariani.** A cast of Mainers (or "Mainiacs" if you prefer) fall in and out of love in ways that only people who live in close proximity to wild moose can do. "A whimsical approach to the joys and perils of romance." –*NY Times.* "Sweet, poignant and witty." –*NY Daily News.* "John Cariani aims for the heart by way of the funny bone." –*Star-Ledger.* [2M, 2W] ISBN: 978-0-8222-2156-2

★ **Mitch Albom's TUESDAYS WITH MORRIE by Jeffrey Hatcher and Mitch Albom, based on the book by Mitch Albom.** The true story of Brandeis University professor Morrie Schwartz and his relationship with his student Mitch Albom. "A touching, life-affirming, deeply emotional drama." –*NY Daily News.* "You'll laugh. You'll cry." –*Variety.* "Moving and powerful." –*NY Post.* [2M] ISBN: 978-0-8222-2188-3

★ **DOG SEES GOD: CONFESSIONS OF A TEENAGE BLOCKHEAD by Bert V. Royal.** An abused pianist and a pyromaniac ex-girlfriend contribute to the teen-angst of America's most hapless kid. "A welcome antidote to the notion that the *Peanuts* gang provides merely American cuteness." –*NY Times.* "Hysterically funny." –*NY Post.* "The *Peanuts* kids have finally come out of their shells." –*Time Out.* [4M, 4W] ISBN: 978-0-8222-2152-4

DRAMATISTS PLAY SERVICE, INC.
440 Park Avenue South, New York, NY 10016 212-683-8960 Fax 212-213-1539
postmaster@dramatists.com   www.dramatists.com

NEW PLAYS

★ **RABBIT HOLE by David Lindsay-Abaire.** Winner of the 2007 Pulitzer Prize. Becca and Howie Corbett have everything a couple could want until a life-shattering accident turns their world upside down. "An intensely emotional examination of grief, laced with wit." *–Variety.* "A transcendent and deeply affecting new play." *–Entertainment Weekly.* "Painstakingly beautiful." *–BackStage.* [2M, 3W] ISBN: 978-0-8222-2154-8

★ **DOUBT, A Parable by John Patrick Shanley.** Winner of the 2005 Pulitzer Prize and Tony Award. Sister Aloysius, a Bronx school principal, takes matters into her own hands when she suspects the young Father Flynn of improper relations with one of the male students. "All the elements come invigoratingly together like clockwork." *–Variety.* "Passionate, exquisite, important, engrossing." *–NY Newsday.* [1M, 3W] ISBN: 978-0-8222-2219-4

★ **THE PILLOWMAN by Martin McDonagh.** In an unnamed totalitarian state, an author of horrific children's stories discovers that someone has been making his stories come true. "A blindingly bright black comedy." *–NY Times.* "McDonagh's least forgiving, bravest play." *–Variety.* "Thoroughly startling and genuinely intimidating." *–Chicago Tribune.* [4M, 5 bit parts (2M, 1W, 1 boy, 1 girl)] ISBN: 978-0-8222-2100-5

★ **GREY GARDENS book by Doug Wright, music by Scott Frankel, lyrics by Michael Korie.** The hilarious and heartbreaking story of Big Edie and Little Edie Bouvier Beale, the eccentric aunt and cousin of Jacqueline Kennedy Onassis, once bright names on the social register who became East Hampton's most notorious recluses. "An experience no passionate theatergoer should miss." *–NY Times.* "A unique and unmissable musical." *–Rolling Stone.* [4M, 3W, 2 girls] ISBN: 978-0-8222-2181-4

★ **THE LITTLE DOG LAUGHED by Douglas Carter Beane.** Mitchell Green could make it big as the hot new leading man in Hollywood if Diane, his agent, could just keep him in the closet. "Devastatingly funny." *–NY Times.* "An out-and-out delight." *–NY Daily News.* "Full of wit and wisdom." *–NY Post.* [2M, 2W] ISBN: 978-0-8222-2226-2

★ **SHINING CITY by Conor McPherson.** A guilt-ridden man reaches out to a therapist after seeing the ghost of his recently deceased wife. "Haunting, inspired and glorious." *–NY Times.* "Simply breathtaking and astonishing." *–Time Out.* "A thoughtful, artful, absorbing new drama." *–Star-Ledger.* [3M, 1W] ISBN: 978-0-8222-2187-6

DRAMATISTS PLAY SERVICE, INC.
440 Park Avenue South, New York, NY 10016 212-683-8960 Fax 212-213-1539
postmaster@dramatists.com   www.dramatists.com